Tavistock Clinic Series

Nick Temple, Margot Waddell (Series Editors)
Published and distributed by Karnac Books

Orders
Tel: +44 (0)20 8969 4454; Fax: +44 (0)20 8969 5585
Email: shop@karnacbooks.com
www.karnacbooks.com

SENT BEFORE MY TIME
A Child Psychotherapist's View of
Life on a Neonatal Intensive Care Unit

Margaret Cohen

KARNAC

LONDON   NEW YORK

First published in 2003 by
H. Karnac (Books) Ltd.
6 Pembroke Buildings, London NW10 6RE
A subsidiary of Other Press LLC, New York

British Library Cataloguing in Publication Data

A C.I.P. for this book is available from the British Library

ISBN: 185575-910-1

10 9 8 7 6 5 4 3 2 1

Edited, designed, and produced by Communication Crafts

Printed and bound in Great Britain by Biddles Ltd, *www.biddles.co.uk*

www.karnacbooks.com

For my family

CONTENTS

ACKNOWLEDGEMENTS

The following chapters were first published as indicated below; they appear here in a revised form:

Chapter 3: in the *Journal of Child Psychotherapy*, 21, No. 2 (August 1995).

Chapter 4 (French translation): in *Le respect*, edited by Catherine Audard (Editions Autrement, 1993), under the title, "Histoires de naissances et de mort".

Chapter 5: in *Integrity in the Public and Private Domains*, edited by Alan Montefiore and David Vines (London: Routledge, 1999), under the title, "A Psychoanalytic View of the Notion of Integrity". Reprinted by permission.

Chapter 10: in *Imprisoned Pain and Its Transformation*, edited by Joan Symington (Karnac, 2000), under the title "Observing Babies and Supporting the Staff".

Extract (p. 210) from "Plurality" by Louis MacNeice: in *Collected Poems*, London & Boston, MA: Faber & Faber, 1966, p. 243. Reprinted by permission of David Higham Associates.

The following figures have been reproduced by permission:

Figure 6 (p. 96). Fra Filippo Lippi: *The Annunciation*. National Gallery, London (copyright National Gallery, London).

Figure 7 (p. 97). Fra Angelico: *The Annunication to Mary*. Corridor of the dormitory, San Marco Monastery, Florence (AKG London / Erich Lessing).

Figure 8 (p. 98). Simone Martini: *Annunciation*. Galleria degli Uffizi, Florence (AKG London).

Figure 9 (p. 99). Piero della Francesca: *Annunciation*. San Francesco, Arezzo (Photo Scala, Florence).

Figure 10 (p. 100). Duccio di Buoninsegna: *The Annunciation*. National Gallery, London (copyright National Gallery, London).

Figure 11 (p. 101). Tintoretto (Jacopo Robusti): *The Annunciation to Mary*. Scuola Grande di San Rocco, Sala Inferiore, Venice (AKG London / Cameraphoto).

Figure 12 (p. 102). Mariotto Albertinelli: *The Visitation*. Galleria degli Uffizi, Florence (AKG London / Rabatti—Domingie).

Figure 13 (p. 103). Giotto di Bondone: *The Visitation of Mary*. Scrovegni Chapel, Padua (AKG London / Cameraphoto).

Figure 14 (p. 104). Piero della Francesca: *Madonna del Parto*. Cappela del Cimitero, Monterchi, Arezzo. (AKG London / Rabatti—Domingie).

Figure 15 (p. 105). Piero della Francesca. *The Madonna of the Protecting Cloak with Saints*. Polyptych from the Compagnia della Misericordia in Sansepolcro (AKG London / Rabatti—Domingie).

Figure 16 (p. 107). Leonardo da Vinci: *The Virgin and Child, with Saint Anne and Saint John the Baptist*. National Gallery, London (copyright National Gallery, London).

Figure 17 (p. 109). Giulio Romano: *The Holy Family and St. Anne with the Christ Child about to be taught to walk*. The Devonshire Collection, Chatsworth (photograph: Photographic Survey, Courtauld Institute of Art).

Figure 18 (p. 111). Masaccio di S. Giovanni: *The Virgin and Child*.

National Gallery, London (copyright National Gallery, London).

Figure 19 (p. 112). Raffaello Santi: *Madonna im Grünen* [Madonna in the Meadow]. Kunsthistorisches Museum, Vienna (by permission of the Kunsthistorisches Museum).

Figure 20 (p. 113). Piero della Francesca: *Mary and Child between Angels and Saint John the Baptist, Bernardin of Siena, Hieronymus, Francis of Assisi, Peter the Martyr & John the Evangelist, and the donor Federigo di Montefeltro.* From the church S. Bernardino in Urbino, Milan; Pinacoteca di Brera, Milan (AKG London / Rabatti–Domingie).

Figure 21 (p. 114). Giovanni Bellini: *Madonna of the Meadow.* National Gallery, London (copyright National Gallery, London).

Figure 22 (p. 115). Piero della Francesca: *The Nativity.* National Gallery, London (copyright National Gallery, London).

Figure 23 (p. 117). Giovanni Bellini: *Mary with Child and Saints.* Chiesa San Zaccaria, Venice (AKG London / Cameraphoto).

Figure 24 (p. 118). Giovanni Bellini: *Madonna with Child and Saints.* Formerly in the Church of S. Giobbe, Venedi; Galleria dellí Accademia, Venice (AKG London / Cameraphoto).

Figure 25 (p. 123). Nicolas Poussin: *The Nurture of Jupiter.* Dulwich Art Gallery, London (reproduced by permission of the Trustees of Dulwich Picture Gallery, London).

SERIES EDITORS' PREFACE

Since it was founded in 1920, the Tavistock Clinic has developed a wide range of developmental approaches to mental health which have been strongly influenced by the ideas of psychoanalysis. It has also adopted systemic family therapy as a theoretical model and a clinical approach to family problems. The Clinic is now the largest training institution in Britain for mental health, providing postgraduate and qualifying courses in social work, psychology, psychiatry, and child, adolescent, and adult psychotherapy, as well as in nursing and primary care. It trains about 1,400 students each year in over 45 courses.

The Clinic's philosophy aims at promoting therapeutic methods in mental health. Its work is based on the clinical expertise that is also the basis of its consultancy and research activities. The aim of this Series is to make available to the reading public the clinical, theoretical, and research work that is most influential at the Tavistock Clinic. The Series sets out new approaches in the understanding and treatment of psychological disturbance in children, adolescents, and adults, both as individuals and in families.

Sent before My Time is at once very personal and also highly professional. It traces, with careful attention to the detail of inner and outer states of being, relationships among colleagues, staff, parents, and babies in the "world apart" of a neonatal intensive care unit. The reader is invited to make the difficult entry into the emotionally fraught, professionally challenging, personally joyous or tragic, always anxious, enclosed worlds of the intensive-care, the high-dependency, and the special-care nurseries.

But the book offers more even than this: its pages evoke a special kind of engagement—engagement with that exquisitely fragile world that forever teeters on the brink of life and death. This rarely understood world is thoroughly understood in these pages—"through internal acquaintance", as the author puts it. This kind of acquaintance is achieved not only through the author's own personal strengths of thought and insight, but through the arduous philosophical and, most immediately, clinical child psychotherapy training that underpins the disciplined capacity to feel deeply and to think clearly at the same time—and the capacity, too, to impart this hard-earned skill to both colleagues and parents.

The infant observational method, pioneered at the Tavistock from the late 1940s, together with psychoanalytically informed work with children and their parents, is shown here both in its contextual specificity and also in its wider application, so that while, indeed, being a uniquely insightful book for healthcare professionals, the personal and professional significances of life and death in the microcosm of this conflictual and traumatic neonatal world extend far beyond the immediate setting—to timeless issues of human and aesthetic value, ones of trust, of cooperation, of integrity, honesty, empathy, and respect.

Nicholas Temple and Margot Waddell
Series Editors

INTRODUCTION

My mother has often told me the story of how I was born during the bombing of Canterbury in May 1942. She has told me that the midwife instructed her that if the bombs started hitting Whitstable, she should roll under the bed with me. She describes how, after this terrible night, the sun rose and lit up the world and she heard the birds singing. I have heard the story, and in some way it has just passed through my mind; at times I have been proud to have been born at that time—as if it lent me some identity. But it has only been of late that I have really thought about what it was like to have lived through that—and then I have to remind myself that I did live through it, that I was that little baby whose mother must have been in such a state of fear and who was so joyful in the morning. My brother has also told me recently that when my mother went off to the nursing home for ten days, he had no idea of where she was going, nor of why. When she returned with me, he was amazed and, he says, jumped out growling, believing that I would like this welcome! Watching one of my granddaughters preparing for the birth of a brother or sister—the thoughts, the plans, the fantasies, the different feelings struggled with—I wonder how he could not have suspected that something was up. Did my mother really omit to tell her 4-year-old son of her imminent absence, the first in his life, and of my forthcoming arrival? Was she silenced by fears of giving birth in wartime?

In some sense I feel that my whole life is poured into this book. And it is essentially a book of thanks. For the past twelve years I have worked in a neonatal intensive care unit—a place that is so full of the stories of people's lives and inevitably reverberates with the staff's experience of life. Hearing mothers talk about their lives has probably made me think more vividly of my mother's story. And then, of course, of my father and grandmother, at home with my brother. My mother feared a German invasion, and this must have been a difficult time to be having a baby, but for me, as a child, the concrete road blocks and the barbed wire were only obstacles to be manoeuvred when going down to the sea to swim. And the street spirit of wartime was not a myth—it was part of everyday life. Sharing out the chickens' eggs, saving every bit of potato peel for chicken-feed, being given meat bones for the dog, the smells, the garden with all its demands, neighbours calling in with their dramas, were all part of the daily regularities. The year was divided into the seasons and into the Church's feasts and fasts. As I got older and went every day by bus through the Kent countryside to the grammar school in Canterbury, I loved to gaze out of the window and watch the changing seasons—that is, when I was not in a panic about homework not done. For the stability, love, devotion, and fun given to us I want to thank my parents, and my grandmother, who was infinitely patient.

Our garden was a tremendously important place for us. My father had a project one summer that we should make the air-raid shelter into a fish-pond with a beautiful rockery around the water. We spent a happy summer heaving breeze blocks, and I still remember the feel of the concrete on my hands. I also remember my father walking between his rows of beans and tomatoes, tending them with his huge competent hands. The chickens had to be looked after, and for some reason my parents were totally tolerant of my love of letting them out and catching them again. There were the beehives to be slightly wary of, and at the bottom of the garden there was the rabbit hutch where Bessie lived. I would look at her and wonder at her life of captivity with some horror. I came to feel that too about my grandmother's life, as I realized that she was no longer leaving the house, then her room, and then her bed. These stories all change over the years as I see them slightly differently. When I was small, I would go with my grandmother to her friend's house. While they drank their tea from thin china teacups, I was allowed to look, with great care, through the large mahogany kaleidoscope that was held on a stand. It was very beautiful, and the wonderfully coloured pieces, like jewels, would fall into new configurations as one rotated the end. I was intrigued by this. If one turned it very slowly, could one control the falling of the pieces? It seemed not. And each new pattern was a wonder of beauty. I think that hearing people's stories is rather like this. A new element enters, and the whole configuration changes. One sees things this way and perhaps never in quite the same way again—unless one gets stuck in rigidly holding on to a point of view. The life that we shared in that community was homogeneous: same religion, same politics, same race, and confident beliefs about what was right and wrong.

My feelings around Bessie the rabbit were serious, and I longed to escape from this idyll into the outside world. Quite by luck, I went to University College London to read philosophy in the early 1960s. Here I was taught by Stuart Hampshire, Richard Wollheim, and Bernard Williams and, later, by Hidé Ishiguro, Myles Burnyeat, and Jerry Cohen—such different people, but all with something in common: their love of ideas. I was astonished at the intellectual freedom that seemed to abound here: no longer an assumption that there were things that you must necessarily think, things that were obviously right or wrong. Our luck was to be taught by people who seemed to take any and every idea seriously, to follow it through, and to see where it went. As the 1960s progressed, every aspect of life was open to question. The Vietnam War became the focus of left-wing thinking. Issues of race and then of gender rocked our ways of thinking about the world. I married into a Montreal Jewish communist family, where arguments about politics and art would rage at every possible opportunity. Stories, beliefs, and customs seemed to be made of such strong stuff that my own roots began to feel rather thin; their depth and richness would only be apparent to me later. In this London life with Jerry Cohen, I gave birth to, and we raised, our three children. I want to thank all of those, teachers and friends, who made life confusing and complicated but also such an exciting and rich time. University College was a harbour of liberal and benign thinking where I found kindness and flexibility.

Under the influence of Richard Wollheim, who was my graduate tutor and good friend, I became interested in the work of Melanie Klein. After the rigours of philosophy, I devoured her books with a sense of recognition. This was no longer thinking of ideas out there, it was about what was going on inside. I went to talk to Mattie Harris at the Tavistock Clinic about doing the Child Psychotherapy training, and after a long conversation she seemed to assume that I would be starting in the autumn term. I did, and for me she was the most wonderful teacher. With her large gardener's hands she seemed to have a capacity to help one to find things in oneself that one did not know were there. As a teacher I have aspired to be like her. Her work-discussion seminars were full of interest and life. I remember the feeling of bursting with ideas. An important element of the training was baby observation. My group was led by Isca Wittenberg. I thought, because I had had children of my own, that this would be easy for me. So I was unprepared for the impact of an experience that was to change my life and is the mainstay of this book. Esther Bick introduced the practice of baby observation to the training of child psychotherapists at the Tavistock Clinic in 1948. Students observe the same baby for an hour a week for two years in its home setting. They learn to observe closely and to write up their observations afterwards. This is a training in observing very carefully and in retaining what has been observed. The experience of watching a baby, in its home, with no other task than to observe, is quite overwhelming. And I would like to thank the family that allowed me into their home to observe their baby as part of my training. What we see is an intensity of experience in the baby far beyond what we make allowances for in everyday life. The impact of the baby on the mother and of the mother on the baby is profound, and as observers we have to struggle with feelings of identification with the baby, or with the mother, or of exclusion. We have to keep an eye on the place of the father, of the siblings, and of grandparents and friends. We learn of the beauty and terrors of observation. We come to realize how much there is in life that we would rather not see, both out there in what we are observing and also in our own responses. Seminars with Isca Wittenberg were extraordinary, as I learnt about how she saw this material. But also, where I had learnt to appreciate disagreement and controversy at University College, with Isca one was forced to put up with—indeed to appreciate—conflict and also to see destructive feelings in oneself. In response to this students gradually began their own psychoanalysis, as did I. And here I want to thank my analyst, Dr Sydney Klein, for his years of patience and insight. It is probably only in retrospect that I really appreciate what he gave me with his devastating sense of humour, keen eye, and bracing kindness.

At the Tavistock Clinic I trained as a child psychotherapist in the Kleinian tradition. This is rooted in the work of Freud and extended with Mrs Klein's interest in the minds and emotional lives of children and, with the beginning of infant observation, of babies. Her thinking has provided a very rich soil for development in the last fifty years and has enabled Kleinians to think about the emotional development of children and adults in terms of their relationships with external figures and with internal figures, which have come to be called "objects". She believed that feelings towards these others can oscillate between self-interest on the one hand and love and concern on the other. The formative arena for this development has been thought of as the relationship of the child with the mother. With ideas about an internal world and how we treat our "objects", Mrs Klein placed psychoanalysis in a moral framework. She believed that children have vivid ideas about their mothers, about their outsides, but also about their insides, and fantasies about what is going on in there. Wilfred Bion extended these ideas to explore the way that a person uses and thinks about his mind and in what ways this can be hindered or interfered with. Freud had come to think that psychoanalysis investigated resistance and transference. This has been extended in the Kleinian tradition, so that analysis is thought of as the tool by means of which the ever-fluctuating relationship of the patient to the therapist can be investigated and the therapist's own states of mind and difficulties can be thought about by the therapist and used to elucidate that relationship. This means that problems that one comes up against in the encounter, instead of being an interference, are seen as the heart of the work. As a child psychotherapist I have been very influenced by the work of Donald Meltzer, who is

central in the development of Kleinian ideas. His help as supervisor is still alive to me after many years.

Soon after I had finished the seven years of training and had
qualified, I began work as a child psychotherapist at the Hospital
for Sick Children, Great Ormond Street. Here I learnt to think
about the child in the family, in its school, and in the community,
and of the child psychotherapist's work as embedded in a multidisciplinary team. For many years I worked on the Mildred Creak
Unit, a children's in-patient psychiatric unit, run at that time by Dr
Bryan Lask, a child psychiatrist. There we struggled to work in a
multidisciplinary way, and I first thought about the operation of a
mental health unit and the impact of the patients on the staff. I felt
that I would not have withstood the vociferous ambivalence towards psychoanalysis at Great Ormond Street without a sense of
my father's loyal pragmatism and my analyst's approach, which
could be summed up in his words: "Well, you are not going to die
of it."

Ten years later I left Great Ormond Street. I worked privately
for three years, but I missed hospital work very much, so when a
job was advertised for a child psychotherapist in a neonatal intensive care unit in a large London hospital, I applied for it. This job
was set up in an unusual way. A group of parents who had had
babies in the unit had formed a charity to raise money in order to
help the unit, but also with the intention of supporting parents
who were now going through that experience. The latter turned
out to be a very complicated enterprise. What was a natural wish
on leaving the unit probably faded as parents became more involved again in their own lives. It turned out that they were good
at raising money, but that supporting other parents was more
difficult. They decided to use the money to employ someone to do
this work. The consultant child psychiatrist, who appears in this
book as Dr Gibbons, and the consultant paediatrician, who appears as Dr Kennedy, had a wider vision of what this job might
involve and argued that a child psychotherapist should be em-
ployed. There was some resistance to this, and when I began the
job I was well aware of it and had to persuade other staff that I was
not a threat to their work. Some parents involved in the charity
had done very remarkable work in supporting other parents both
before and after I was in post. I enjoyed working with them and

learnt much through hearing about their encounters with parents on the unit. Other parents were involved in raising money and organizing many different kinds of events. The charity provided money for two years, after which the NHS funded the job. I think that there may have been some difficulties between me and the charity. When I began work on the unit, I was overwhelmed by the nature of the work and the stress under which the staff operated. I became very protective of the staff at all levels. There was inevitably an element of criticism in the charity's work: that the parents were having to provide the support that they had not themselves been given when they had had babies in the unit, that they were sorting it out, improving it psychologically and physically. They may have felt deserted by me as I disappeared into the unit—and I probably failed to remain properly in touch with them. I want to thank the charity for the initial two years of my work and for its vision in supporting the venture. This book is a token of that gratitude. It is, naturally, addressed to doctors, nurses, and other professionals who are working in intensive care units, but I hope that others may be interested, and I have tried to make the setting and the medical terms accessible.

As must be clear, this introduction is by way of an acknowledgement. I want to thank the unit—that is, the nurses, the cleaners, the receptionists, the succession of junior doctors, and the consultant paediatricians—for allowing me to live among them for so many years, for sharing their ideas with me, and for their comradeship. I would particularly thank the consultants for their generous support and for the ongoing discussion of cases. I thank the speech and language therapist, the social worker, and the chaplain. I also want to thank my support team: the child psychiatrists, the child psychotherapist, social workers, the psychologists, and the secretary. Alongside the staff, I wish to thank the patients with whom I have worked and who have at times put up with my clumsiness. I am surprised and moved at how open patients are in telling me about their lives and have a strong sense of what a great privilege it is to listen.

This book is about the triangular interchange between babies, parents, and staff in a NICU. My view is that the experience of the babies' prematurity is traumatic for each of these, and that this influences whatever goes on in such a unit. I am not suggesting that such units should not exist, but that we do need to recognize how traumatic the experience of them can be, otherwise we do not understand many of the situations that we find ourselves in. The babies' experience is so hard for us to imagine, and it is so much easier not to imagine it, because it is often painful, but if we dismantle our ability to think, this affects the way we treat each other and our patients. Our ethical frameworks often turn out to be inadequate, and we have painfully to rethink our values. The following chapters describe and theorize this. My point of view is very much formed by the experiences and education that I have been describing.

I want to thank Alberto Hahn for years of interesting supervision, encouragement, and friendship; Elinor Wedeles for her warmth and lively imagination of babies; Wilhelmina Kraemer-Zurné and Sebastian Kraemer for their help with the text and for their belief that I could write this book; Alan Montefiore and Catherine Audard for asking me to write for philosophical collections papers, which are the basis of chapters 4 and 5, on Respect and Integrity; Heather Mackinnon and Ed Broadhurst, without whom none of this would have happened, and whose ways of thinking I shall always value; Jerry Cohen for his careful reading of the text, his generous enthusiasm, and for a lifelong friendship; Gillie Kennedy for sharing with me her passion for baby observation; Sevin and Maurice Whitby and Armand Jacoubovitch for their help and enthusiasm; David Wolton for steadfast and humorous support and love in all that I do. My great thanks go to my children, who make my life rich and surprising—I thank them for their individuality and for their love and imaginative help.

And so I dedicate this book with love to my family—in particular to my parents, Aubrey and Florence, to Jerry Cohen, to my children, Gideon, Miriam, and Sarah, and to their partners and children, my grandchildren, and to my husband, David Wolton—to these, my comrades through life.

Note

For the sake of confidentiality the names of all patients and staff have been changed. In non-specific instances, I have used the masculine pronoun for all doctors and all babies, and the feminine pronoun for all nurses.

SENT BEFORE MY TIME

... The wants of an infant are at first made intelligible by instinctive cries, which after a time are modified in part unconsciously, and in part, as I believe, voluntarily as a means of communication,— by the unconscious expression of the features,— by gestures and in a marked manner by different intonations,— lastly by words of a general nature invented by himself, then of a more precise nature from those which he hears; and these latter are acquired at a wonderfully quick rate. An infant understands to a certain extent, and as I believe at a very early period, the meaning or feelings of those who tend him, by the expression of their features.

Charles Darwin, "A Biographical Sketch of an Infant", *Mind*, Volume 2, Issue 7 (July 1877), pp. 285–294

CHAPTER ONE

The setting

> . . . sent before my time
> Into this breathing world, scarce half made up
>
> Shakespeare, *Richard III*, Act I, Scene 1

One enters the neonatal intensive care unit (NICU) through a locked door. From the very beginning one has strong thoughts: this is a world apart—some privileged people have cards that open the door, others have to wait until they have identified themselves. It is a world to which one has to gain entry. There is a sense that what is inside is fragile and that what is outside may be dangerous. Sometimes doctors who occasionally have to run quickly with babies from the labour ward to the NICU are worried about gaining entry fast enough. In the time that I have been working on the NICU, entry to the unit has become more difficult—and I think this is to do with a stronger perception that we live in a dangerous world. I have often thought that there is something womb-like about the unit: it is apart from the rest of the hospital, hard to gain entry to, and very enclosed.

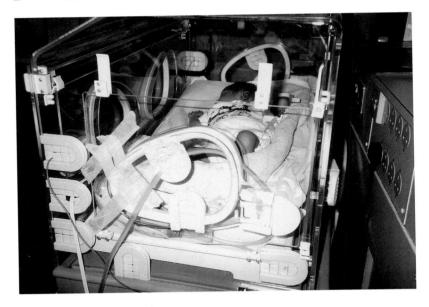

Figure 1.   Incubator.

Once inside, one is encouraged to take off one's coat and to wash one's hands. Here again is the idea of danger: one may be bringing in germs from outside. Very soon one sees the big windows of the nurseries ahead. The unit had two and, more recently, has three nurseries: the hot, the cool, and the intermediate—although to any healthy adult these are all rather too warm for comfort. The more official titles are the intensive care, the high-dependency, and the special care nurseries.

The premature babies often come to the unit in quite a dramatic way. There may have been word that a baby is expected, particularly if there are twins or triplets. The unit will have tried to prepare itself, and a team will have gone to the labour ward to be ready for the baby. The baby may have needed a lot of work to resuscitate him at birth, and he may have been born by Caesarean section. Whatever his story, the mother can often not hold her baby before he is hurried away. These babies may be as early as 22 weeks' gestation and weigh as little as 500 grams. Very-low-birth-weight babies—that is, babies weighing less than 1,500 grams—

account for 2% of all live births, and more than one in ten of these will be left with some major disability. Once in the unit, babies will be fitted up with whatever is needed to sustain their life. Mothers come to the unit from the postnatal ward as soon as they can to see their baby; if they cannot come, a nurse will bring them a photograph of their new baby. Some babies coming to the NICU are not premature but full-term babies in some kind of difficulty.

The intensive care nursery can take up to ten babies but will then be very crowded. The babies lie on platforms just above adult waist height. These platforms may be surrounded by a Perspex fence to prevent the baby from slipping out, or they may be covered by a Perspex incubator. These incubators have port-holes in the sides for the staff to put their hands through to care for the baby. The quality of the incubators has vastly improved over the last twelve years. An ultraviolet light may shine on the baby to counteract jaundice, and in this case the baby will wear a mask to protect his eyes.

Surrounding each bed is a jumble of equipment, joined to the baby by several leads. These are attached to the babies' arms, legs,

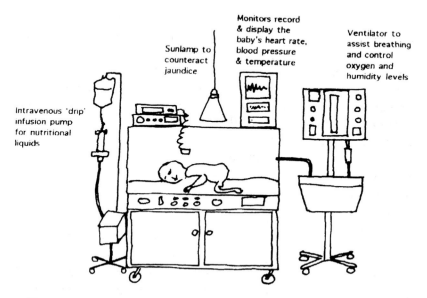

Figure 2.   Incubators and monitors: a diagrammatic layout.

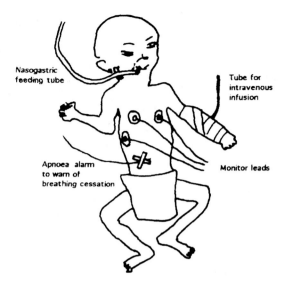

Nasogastric
feeding tube

Tube for
intravenous
infusion

Apnoea alarm
to warn of
breathing cessation

Monitor leads

Figure 3.   Tubes and monitor leads.

and trunk. Sometimes taped to their arms and legs there are tubes that can be quite heavy and presumably give the baby an odd sensation. The babies breathe artificially by means of a ventilator that is strapped to their nose or mouth. They are mostly fed intravenously. There are bright lights overhead, which occasionally get turned down. The beds are very close together, and nurses are often working on the babies. They have high stools to sit on. There is the constant noise of alarms going off as the babies' oxygen requirements are monitored. The nurses are aware that the babies need less stimulation, and they make an effort to instigate quiet times in the day—but these often have to be interrupted if the doctors are available then to work on the babies. In this nursery the parents can sometimes hold their babies, but this takes cooperation from a nurse, who has to arrange the leads and make sure that all the equipment is safe. Nurses vary in how much they encourage mothers to do this. Some nurses have noticed that some babies need less oxygen when they are being held by their mothers. Some nurses will also encourage the mothers to hold their babies against their own skin.

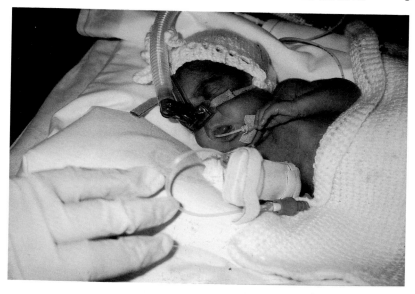

Figure 4.   Baby on ventilation.

The babies graduate from this nursery to the intermediate, or high-dependency, nursery. Here the care is not so intensive. The babies may be in a headbox (a Perspex box covering the baby's head and shoulders and conserving oxygen supply); they are probably being fed nasogastrically, and the mothers will be providing more of their care. At the end of this nursery there is an isolation cubicle for any baby who may have an infection that is dangerous to the other babies.

From the intermediate nursery the babies go to the cool nursery. They may be "in air"—that is, breathing naturally—or they

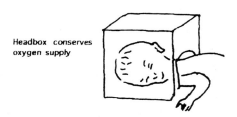

Headbox conserves oxygen supply

Figure 5.   Headbox.

may be "in a trickle of oxygen". It seems that many preterm babies find it very hard to give up this trickle of oxygen and to breathe unaided, and this is often an obstacle to their going home. The trickle comes through a tube that is taped to the baby's face and ends at the nostril. There is something wonderful when this can be taken off and the mother can see the baby's face unencumbered for the first time. The babies here may still be being fed nasogastrically, or the mothers may be beginning to try to breast-feed or bottle-feed them. Many mothers heroically express their milk for weeks or even months, so that their own milk can be put down the tube, and also to keep the flow going so that when they have the chance to breast-feed, their milk is still there. In this nursery usually the babies lie in little Perspex cots, where they look cosier and less vulnerable. It is much easier for the parents to take them out, although the nurses may still have to help them to manoeuvre the leads. The mothers gradually take over the care of their babies when they visit, until their baby is ready to go home.

After the birth the mother will be able to stay on the postnatal ward for a few days, but she will then have to go home and come to visit her baby in the NICU. The unit is open 24 hours a day to parents, but it is very traumatic for mothers to have to leave the hospital without their babies. There is, on the unit, a small room used by the mothers to sit in, where they can stay overnight, but this is only allowed in special circumstances. All mothers "room in" with their baby for at least one night before taking him home. If a baby is very ill or dying, the parents often camp out in this room. Sometimes parents live far away; this can happen if a woman gives birth early while away from home, or, in these days of scarcity of beds, the baby may have had to have been brought from far away because of a lack of local resources. This is then extremely difficult for parents and sometimes they are allowed, unofficially, to stay in the Nurses' Home.

The atmosphere on the unit is friendly but quite hectic. The doctors are overworked and often tired. Nursing suffers chronically from understaffing. To a stranger the hi-tech equipment is rather daunting, and the flashing lights and alarm signals can be unnerving. On the whole, the atmosphere of the cool nursery is much more relaxed, but even here there may be a baby who is no longer in danger but who is sick or seriously handicapped.

Whereas the mothers in the hot nursery are usually extremely frightened, in the cool nursery they may not be so terrified, but they are often worn out with the weeks or months of visiting the NICU. Their babies are usually more stable, and mothers often become more complaining and angry—as if they can only then afford to have these feelings. They may also be feeling torn apart by the conflicting commitments to the baby and to home. This book does not attend to the difficulties experienced by the new baby's brothers and sisters, but I am very aware that these can be serious, that life at home is very disrupted, and that in an ideal world we should make more provision for siblings to visit the hospital.

The staffing of the unit has changed somewhat over the twelve years that I have been working there, but in essence it is the same. There are consultant paediatricians, registrars who stay for four months, senior house officers who stay for six months, a nurse manager, sisters, staff nurses, and more junior nurses, a reception-ist, and cleaners. The unit is further served by a social worker, a speech and language therapist, child psychotherapists, child psy-chiatrists, a health visitor, and a chaplain. There is a nurse man-ager who runs the unit and above her a hierarchy of managers in the hospital. The unit meets once a week to discuss each baby both medically and from a psychosocial point of view. There is a weekly business meeting to discuss the working of the unit. And there is a weekly staff support meeting. In addition, there are various teach-ing and training sessions.

Throughout this book I refer to the trauma of neonatal inten-sive care. I think that the experience of the babies is traumatic: they are often in pain, they cannot be picked up by their mother for the first few weeks, they are not living at home but in a high-tech unit. For the parents the experience is also traumatic: they cannot take charge of their babies, they cannot begin the process of finding their way to bring up their child, to claim it as theirs; they have to stand by, impotent and in public. It is traumatic for the staff to bear witness to all of this pain. So there is a triangle between the babies, the parents, and the staff, which is fraught with difficulty. But the atmosphere on the unit is rather ordinary. The staff work here every day: this is their life, their norm, and so the extraordinary character of what is going on tends to get lost. When one reminds staff of it, they can be quite baffled. But unless they keep a fresh vision of how unusual and distressing much of what goes on is, they cannot reach out and understand the babies and parents. Of course, the staff need to get on with their work, so they often prefer parents who do not make a fuss. I often feel that we should be worried about these parents and keep in mind that sometimes it is healthy and positive to be making a fuss and to be upset.

CHAPTER TWO

Two ways of seeing

... the traces of the storyteller cling to the story the way the handprints of the potter cling to the clay vessel.

Walter Benjamin, *The Storyteller*, 1999

When I applied for the child psychotherapy post at the neonatal intensive care unit of a large inner-city hospital, the part of the job description that caught my attention was that the post-holder would be expected to articulate the babies' experience. I understood that I would also be required to be available to mothers, to fathers, to extended families, and to staff, that my job would be to listen and to try to understand their feelings. Although these latter things were difficult, I had some ideas about how to do them, some experience to fall back on. I was not too surprised that I felt rather superfluous in a busy unit, that I often wished I were a doctor and could be clear about what I should be doing and could do something useful, without feeling so full of ignorance and impotence. These are states of mind that psychoanalytically trained therapists are familiar with and learn to tolerate. But articulating these babies' experience—that was something different. I rather fancied myself as knowing about babies; after all, I had had three of my own, and I had also done a two-year baby observation as part of my training and had supervised others doing such observations here in London and for many years in Italy. But these babies on the NICU I found hard to watch. I wondered what they were feeling and, dare one say, thinking. One doctor said to me: "We do such dreadful things to them, I just hope that they forget." Whether or not the baby forgets the experience, I wondered if it was ever going to be possible to imagine what the babies' experience might be. I decided I had to sit and observe the babies and to get to know them, to know which baby belonged to which mother, and so on.

Which brings me to what I want to discuss: two different ways of looking at the same things. The way we describe these two ways depends partly on our prejudices, but also on our task—for instance rational or non-rational, practical or imaginative, reality-based or fantasy-based, sane or insane. We can all see things in different ways but we vary in our positions along these spectra, and we vary in what we prefer to concentrate on. So it seems to me that medical people in a work situation like the NICU have to emphasize the practical, the rational, the real, the sane, in order to get on with their work, while the psychotherapist will be more aware of the non-rational, the imaginative, fantasy, and the insane—and thinking and describing in this way seems akin to storytelling. Child psychiatrists at their best try to bridge the gap between these different ways of seeing.

I wondered what acknowledgement the non-rational and the imaginative could have in the unit. Admitted to or not, they must be there. Birth is one of the most powerful events in human life. Art and religion have struggled with its mystery throughout the centuries. We know that people exhibit powerful and surprising reactions and behaviour around birth—that they often "do not feel themselves". We know also that new mothers are usually in unstable states of mind and are even given special dispensation in the law courts. But how can we think about this, and should it make any difference to us? One mother told me how she had imagined her labour and childbirth: there would be a darkened room, with one well-known and friendly midwife, who would maintain a peaceful atmosphere. Instead of which she was able to count, at one point, no fewer than fifteen people in the room. There were spotlights directed on parts of her that she had always regarded as intensely personal. She was surrounded by cold, hard instruments whose function it did not take much imagination to guess at. She knew that all this was necessary, but for the time being she did not want any contraceptive advice, as she thought that she would not be having sex for quite a while.

So there is this issue of privacy; this intensely private experience—a mother and baby getting to know each other—has by necessity been made public. I do not think that it is exaggerating to describe this invasion of privacy as traumatic. Here is the story of one young woman, her baby, and her family as she told it to me and as I observed it.

* * *

I heard that there was a new baby in the unit: a 24-weeker. This means that the baby had been born 16 weeks early. Coming into the nursery, I saw a young man looking at the equipment round an incubator. I went up to him and explained who I was. I asked him how his wife was and said that if either of them would like to talk to me, I was available. I sensed that he wanted to get back to studying the machinery around his baby, so I went on my way.

When the baby was one week old, I spoke to the mother, who, I discovered, was called Mrs "Kelly". She told me that her husband had already spoken to me, and I remembered the young man by the incubator. She said that she was a Protestant, her husband a Catholic, and at present she was living at her mother's so that her other little boy, who was one year old, would be looked after while she visited the hospital. There were difficulties with her husband's parents, who did not accept her. She said that she was more in touch with feelings than her husband was, that she sometimes longed to be cuddled and told that she was lovely. She talked about what she wanted to do if her baby died. She would take out all the tubes and hold him for as long as she wanted. Then she would go home, not see anyone, maybe never be able to see her parents again.

Two days later Mrs Kelly burst into tears as soon as she saw me. She told me that the baby, who was now named "Ewan", had suffered a setback. She was desperate for a cigarette, something for herself. She told me that this pregnancy had been a mistake, she had not had her coil checked because she was so busy with her first baby, and she had become pregnant. She had had bleeding during the pregnancy. They had never found the coil; maybe it was still inside her.

After another three days I saw Mrs Kelly, and again she immediately began to cry. The session with me was a long diatribe against the doctors and nurses, and about how difficult things were at her mother's, because her mother was assuming that she was going to be sterilized. She had wanted a granddaughter and now she was hoping for one from her daughter-in-law, who was pregnant. Mrs Kelly was hurt by her mother's excitement and bitterly felt the loss of her own pregnancy. She wanted to be cruel to her mother. She said that she would like to drive away from all of this to be in a bubble somewhere. She was envious of her sister who was young and carefree, whereas she was tied down to nappies and a breast pump.

At this point I thought I had better get to know this baby better, so I sat by his cot and watched him.

Ewan was lying on his back in the incubator. His skin was red and looked parchment-thin and very dry. His arms and legs, particularly his thighs, were very wrinkled. His stomach was rather bloated, so the skin looked particularly thin and dry there. His eyes were closed. His mouth was bunged up with the ventilator. There was a heavy plaster holding the tubes in place on his right hand and a lighter bandage on his left arm. More tubes were plastered to his legs. His nakedness felt quite shocking, and in the middle of all this equipment his penis looked obvious and vulnerable. All around in the unit there was the constant noise of a radio, machinery, and bleepers, a dull light, and flashing signs.

Ewan was lying with his knees splayed open. He moved his legs up and down. A nurse came to turn his oxygen supply up. He stretched his arms up and suddenly moved his legs. Each breath seemed very pronounced. He moved his legs and was then still. He turned one hand, then moved his legs and was still. He moved his arm, then head, and then convulsively his legs. He was still and then jumped. He stretched his left leg out and then the right, then rested his legs out straight, and then with a convulsive breath drew them up, and then he was still, with his legs splayed open. He made a sucking movement. Then closed his mouth for two seconds and opened it. His legs and arms moved. His left leg went up and down. Then he was still. His tongue moved around his mouth. Both his legs were drawn up and were then still. His breathing suddenly became more body-shaking. His penis moved with his breathing, and a spurt of urine shot out. His legs moved, and his breathing became shallower. Then his arms moved convulsively.

I felt for him, wishing he could be still for more than a moment. I observed for a few more minutes and then could not bear it any more. I looked around the unit, taking time off. Then I began to observe again. After a while, I wondered if all the babies were so restless. I felt very distractable and longed for some mothers to arrive on the unit. I thought that they could take care of the babies, or alternatively I could take care of one of them.

A week later, when Ewan was nearly a month old, I saw Mrs Kelly. She said she felt guilty about feeling happy on the way to the hospital. She wondered how she could be happy when Ewan was going through all this. She thought that she should be by his side and protect him. She hated anyone looking at him, particularly her family. I wondered if she looked at him to keep him alive. I thought that she was terrified of having hostile feelings towards Ewan, and so these feelings were split off into others; she behaved as if they had the evil eye and she did not want them to look at him.

At about this time Mrs Kelly told me that she and her husband were rowing a lot. Ewan had a mask on as part of his ventilation, and his parents hated this because they could not see his face, and also because they felt that it distressed him. Furthermore, she told me that she was going to have a scan to try to locate the coil lodged inside her.

Very soon after this, Ewan developed meningitis and was having fits, although this was masked by the phenobarbitone. Mother and father were both tremendously upset and came to the session together. Mother felt that she could not look at Ewan any more, in case he was fitting. She was also very upset by the bad wound he had from the tubes in his hand. She knew that this would leave a permanent scar. She did not want to visit him any more, she could not bear to sit by the incubator. At the end of the session, they said they had become terrified that they might carry away the meningitis and give it to their other child.

A week later, Mrs Kelly told me about her identification with Ewan—that when he stopped breathing, she could not breathe; that when he was having some intervention, she found herself backing out the door. She said that she went off into her own little world far away. I wondered whether Ewan was doing the same with his bradycardias. During this session I felt quite overwhelmed by her, and it was only afterwards that I thought that she was defending herself against thoughts of Ewan dying. I felt that I had let her down by not understanding this at the time. At around this time Mrs Kelly was to have the coil dug out of the wall of her womb. There was a question about whether this would affect her fertility.

Mrs Kelly told me about a mad woman who had wandered into the unit, and how she could not bear this when Ewan was so ill. (This was before security on the unit had become tight.) She had had a bad row with her mother, and she felt that nobody understood what she was going through. She became obsessed with buying a double pram at this time—one that would take both her children. She also thought a lot about having another baby. At the same time she talked more about what a battle Ewan was having, so much more than any of the other babies in the unit. Both parents became very critical of the care on the unit. They felt they knew Ewan so well that they could see that wrong decisions were sometimes made. They worried about leaving him when they did not feel that he was in good hands.

When Ewan was 2½ months old, he could not be fed, because there were no undamaged veins left to get the TPN (total parenteral nutrition) line into. It was decided that the registrar would try to get a line into his skull. There was considerable worry about his weak state due to malnutrition. When I went to see him, Ewan was lying very still. Every now and then he sucked the tube in his mouth. His face was fat and puffy, with many tubes. A doctor came to take a blood sample. Ewan became agitated, flayling his arms around in a warding-off fashion. He screwed up his face. The nurse said that it would take him an hour to settle, and that she felt he was desperate for a cuddle. She stroked him and talked to him, and it seemed that the tension ebbed out of him with her caresses. She said that sometimes he hated to be touched—you could see that from his face, and it was horrible to watch. She went away, and Ewan began his frantic movements again, writhing and squirming, it seemed, to try to get rid of something.

At this time Mrs Kelly was very depressed, and then the parents heard from the doctors that there was a high probability that Ewan would be blind. They were both stunned. They wandered in and out of the room where we were meeting, as if they did not know where to put themselves. They talked about their feelings of guilt. They wondered what they had been fighting for, and whether Ewan would thank them for it. They both felt that it was very hard to look at him.

Ewan's feeding improved at around 3 months. He had had the laser treatment for his eyes, but the outcome would not be known for several weeks. This treatment leaves the eyes very bruised, and one consultant said that it would feel like being kicked in the eyes. Mrs Kelly had left her mother's house and gone back to live at home, and she would now only visit in the evening. Both parents were rather manic.

After three weeks, it seemed that the eye treatment had probably not been successful. Mrs Kelly was enraged with her husband, because he felt that it would have been better if Ewan had died. She said that she would fight for him. I felt that, with her rage, she was warding off depression or terror and perhaps her own wishes that Ewan would die. I was impressed by the similarity between her and Ewan—they both seemed to fight on in the face of terrible odds.

* * *

So what are we to make of all this "material", as psychotherapists call it? Can we articulate the experience of this mother and her baby—that is, give a true and even useful account in words of some things for which there may be no agreed meaning?

While I was thinking about how to write about this, I came across a story in Walter Benjamin's *The Storyteller*. This story was originally told by Herodotus in his *Histories* and tells of Psammenitus, King of the Egyptians, who was defeated by Cambyses, the King of the Persians. In order to humiliate his prisoner, King Cambyses made Psammenitus stand by the side of the road along which the Persians displayed their prisoners. Thus Psammenitus was forced to witness the enslavement of his daughter, who walked by with a pitcher on her head. His son was also led past to be executed. Psammenitus kept his eyes on the ground and uttered not a word. Soon afterwards Psammenitus recognized one of his old servants in the train of prisoners, and only then did he express his grief, beating himself and wailing loudly. I find this a haunting story, and, as Benjamin points out, we are left with the question: why did he show his grief only then? Benjamin argues that this is the mark of true narrative, that it carries with it a potential—for instance, a potential for a whole variety of explanations and the inexhaustible meanings of how Psammenitus shows his grief. Scholars have given different interpretations of why Psammenitus broke down at this point, but none of these is conclusive. Benjamin says: "... this story from ancient Egypt is still capable after thousands of years of arousing astonishment and thoughtfulness".

I think we are left in a similar situation with the story of Mrs Kelly and her baby. The explanations and meanings are varied and inexhaustible. The psychotherapist's task is to stay with all this uncertainty, to seek meaning, but to understand that we are never going to exhaust it or be sure of it. Then we have to consider whether our view of things is of any use to those around us. Our job is not to give a definitive statement. Perhaps it is to allow emotion and perhaps in the story of Psammenitus we might think that there was something about his relationship with his old servant, someone who was familiar and domestic, which at last enabled him to weep, but we are left in uncertainty about this and knowing that this is just the interpretation that we choose.

I would offer these thoughts about Mrs Kelly's story. Here we have a young woman tormented by guilt about what her attempts to stop conception have done to her precious baby. She wonders whether she will now be punished for wishing that she were not pregnant and be banned from future creativity. Perhaps in her mind her good mother has turned into the spiteful witch mother of our nightmares, keen to keep all the riches, such as future grand-children, for herself and attacking her daughter's sexuality and fertility. Perhaps she is both preparing herself for the loss of her baby but also, with the purchase of the pram, magically keeping him alive. She is holding on to him desperately with her eyes, holding him in life and trying to protect him from the evil eyes of others. I wonder where her anger and maybe even her wish for him to die, have gone—and I think they may have gone into her mother, the doctors, the negligent nurses, and, latterly, her hus-band. Perhaps at times this projection does not feel so secure, and she cannot look at her baby because she is afraid that he will see hostile thoughts expressed in her eyes.

And the baby? What is his story? I wonder whether the coil was an irritation in the womb, which then threatened to eject him and finally did throw him out too early into the world, where he ex-changed the comfort of the placenta for the pain and discomfort of the tubes and pumps. Perhaps he brought this experience with him in his endless writhings, into a world where there is no comfort or peace. I wonder whether he is aware of his mother's eyes that hold on to him; and what his experience of the mask is when it is in place—whether he feels cut off from the tenuous link with his watching parents. Perhaps his bradycardias act as a defence that lowers his oxygen levels and therefore the levels of his sensation and take him off to a secret place of his own, like the place his mother dreams off to, where the pain is less. And his fits, like his mother's rages, may be an evacuation of unbearable feelings. I wonder why this baby has grown cysts on his eyes, thus ruining his vision, and whether this is to sever a link with the external world, which has proved too painful. Perhaps it has become too difficult for him to hold on to the external world. The laser treat-ment might have felt like a searing counter-attack from the outside and have led to such a severe bradycardia two hours later. Perhaps this baby is both ready to fight for life and drawn to give himself up to oblivion.

Whatever construction we build from the material, it does seem that both the participants and the observers are likely to be scarred by this experience and to feel at times that it is going to drive us mad, like the woman who, according to Mrs Kelly, is invading the unit and threatening her baby's safety. Relief comes when the nurse is so in touch with Ewan and caresses him, and he can momentarily be still. When I watched Ewan, I sometimes felt overwhelmed by grief and experienced an unbearable combination of willing him to fight and to live and wishing he could slip away into peace, be allowed to let go and give up this terrible battle.

Postscript

A few months after beginning work on the unit I was asked by the paediatricians to tell them about my work. The paper I wrote formed the basis of this chapter. When I read it to them, they were interested and asked many questions. Then Dr Kennedy, a consultant paediatrician, said that it was interesting to hear in so much detail about this family because it had seemed to the doctors to be one of the less problematic cases; it was clear medically what should be done, and the parents seemed to be coping well. So, from a medical point of view it was quite straightforward, but from my point of view there was a whole world here to consider.

CHAPTER THREE

Twins

> ... the daylight fades
> To dusk and a new moon is in the sky,
> And knitting up their brows they squinnied at us
> Like an old tailor at the needle's eye.

Dante, The Divine Comedy: Inferno, Canto XV

A t the heart of unit life are the babies. But it is often hard to view them as babies—that is, as small human beings. A junior doctor once told me that the babies made no impact on him, he just did his job; later, however, he said that he was having bad nightmares about them and asked whether he was "going nuts".

So at the heart of our working life there are the babies, and we often do not want to see them. Doctors may cover the baby while they take a limb to try to insert a line. Nurses are more in touch, but even they are sometimes more involved with the machinery than with the baby. The very small babies have their eyes closed. Gradually they begin to open them: what is this world like that they have come into? There is always the terrible fear that a very premature baby may end up blind because of the high levels of oxygen used to help the babies breathe. So sight and seeing are problematic issues.

It is against this background that from time to time I have decided to observe a particular baby regularly during its stay in the NICU. Because I too have my reservations about letting the impact of these babies hit me, I often find reasons not to do this, and it is very easy for me to fill my time with other things. It is easier to talk to mothers, fathers, or staff, however traumatic this may be, than to sit and watch a baby. There is the difficulty of looking at a baby, who may be in pain, or be uncomfortable, or who may have deformities of one kind or another. There is the further difficulty of entering this baby's world, of trying to make sense of their movements and of this experience. Doctors sometimes argue that the movements of a baby are involuntary, springing from an immature central nervous system. Is it crazy to be watching them? Certainly the reaction to one's doing so is that one may well be for the birds. "Maggie, what are you doing? . . . Oh, you're bird-watching again." And it is not just out there—inside I feel that perhaps I am deluded, or that I need some learned authoritative guide, internal or external, to interpret for me what is going on. I find myself in the middle of the philosophical debate about consciousness. Is there consciousness behind these movements, am I searching for a world of meaning that is not there, am I putting questions that are pseudo-questions? I cling to my intuition that these babies have their own consciousness and legitimate experience and to my psychoanalytic belief that we as adults carry our infantile experience inside us and that the terrors accompanying this are what hinders us from entering more imaginatively into the babies' experience. I think the apprehension of these babies, unheld sometimes for weeks and often in pain, is so excruciating that the goodness and strength of our own internal world is put under great stress—hence my casting around for philosophical and psychoanalytic support. I think this is one explanation for the high level of irritability often found on the unit: the pull into paranoid-schizoid states is very strong.

Along with the denigration by the staff of what I am doing, there is, of course, the accompanying idealization and then anger at the choice of baby to be observed. "Why are you so interested in that baby?" And I begin to worry whether the baby will suffer because I have chosen it, or that others will be neglected.

The method of observing I have used is adapted from my Tavistock training. When I watch the very small babies lying alone in their incubators, I take notes as I watch, not feeling myself capable of remembering the almost unceasing movements that the babies display and of writing these up later. Once the babies are being held by their mothers, fathers, or nurses, I observe, and I write up my observations afterwards. I also inevitably have a mixed role—I cannot only be an observer. I am the unit child psychotherapist, and sometimes I intervene or give my view. But I see my job primarily as some kind of container for experience on the unit. I have wondered whether my decision to take notes as I watch is in order to distance myself, to give myself something to do in the face of the raw, unprotected experience of the baby, and I think there may be some truth in that.

The story that follows is about two particular babies—twins. I first heard about them at the psychosocial meeting—a weekly meeting of the unit staff to update ourselves on the medical condition of each baby and to discuss the baby and family in a multidisciplinary way. I learnt there that they were the first babies of a 40-year-old mother, that they had come *in utero* from another hospital, and that they were 27 weeks' gestation—that is, they were 13 weeks early. The babies had been born and were brought immediately to the NICU; the mother was then on the postnatal ward, several floors up from the unit. I decided to visit the mother up on the ward, and later I asked the consultant whether he had any objection to my asking the parents if I could observe the babies. Part of my reason for choosing these twins was that their prospects sounded quite hopeful. I felt so overwhelmed by the pain of some mothers and babies that I had observed and written about that I needed to follow something through that was less dramatically traumatic.

* * *

I first saw Mr and Mrs "Smith" on the postnatal ward two days after the twins were born. They had a small room off the main ward—a concession often made to mothers who are unable to have their babies with them, so that they are not so bombarded by the sight of other mothers with their newborn babies. Mr and Mrs Smith were sitting together talking when I came in; she, in particular, looked very composed. They were very welcoming to me as I explained who I was, and they immediately launched into a description of the previous few days. It was very impressive to hear how they shared in this story-telling, each allowing the other to speak. They told me how Mrs Smith had gone into labour at their local hospital. She was moved to our hospital because the twins would need intensive care. Both parents said that the worst part had been waiting for the ambulance. Mother said that the twins had been in two separate amniotic sacs. She described the girl as having been on top. She had kicked a lot in the womb; she had kicked her brother, who was underneath and was described by his mother as more of a wriggler. Sometimes the girl would come up so high that her mother had to move her down. Later she described her as trying to climb up to her heart. The mother felt that her daughter had bullied her brother. The waters of his amniotic sac had broken and brought on labour. I wondered whether mother felt that the girl was responsible.

Mother had had an epidural, and after birth the twins were taken down to the intensive care unit. Mr Smith described his son being born and being whisked aside for resuscitation. He wanted to go with him but also to be beside his wife for the next baby coming out. Right at the beginning he thus experienced the pull in two directions that he was to continue to find so difficult. As the girl was born, she grasped his finger, which he had offered her. He found this immensely moving and felt very close to her. Father said that he was finding it very hard to leave the hospital and go home at night. Mother described feeling closer to the boy, father to the girl. I made an appointment to see them in two days' time, again in their room.

I arrived as arranged to find that they had had a very bad time the day before. The boy's lung had collapsed, and he had to have "a thing going into his chest". The girl was on a ventilator. Mother described liking to talk to the twins and also stroking them. Father said that he felt silly talking to them. They spoke a little about their families of origin. Mrs Smith said that her mother lived in Australia, that she had four sisters, a brother who had died before she was born, and a premature sister who also had died. They were both very keen to talk, saying that it was very helpful. Mother went on to say that she felt that the twins already had personalities of their own. This enabled me to ask if I could observe them, as I was very interested in twins, and they both quickly agreed. Father said that I should observe them as much as I could and stroke them. I said that I would not do that, since that was their job. I added that if at any point they did not want me to observe any more, they should tell me so. They said that they had been quite upset the day before because the girl had been jumpy and they thought she was uncomfortable. Mother added, however, that she was a great fighter and that they were both very strong. She said that the boy opened his eyes whenever he heard her. I felt that the discussion about observation had allowed her to talk about her own observations.

Father seemed to be carrying a lot of the emotional pain involved in this crisis, perhaps being more in touch than his wife with the babies' experience. He felt for their distress and was affronted by it. Mother seemed to be working hard to keep her feelings at bay. The one thing that really upset her was the crying at night on the postnatal ward of the abandoned baby of a drug addict.

I saw the parents again the following week, when the twins were 8 days old. "Daniel", as the boy was now called, had had a bad weekend. Both parents were very upset. The doctors said that Daniel had some kind of infection, and the feeding lines had to come out. Mother reported that he looked awful, and that she had fallen apart in the parents' room. Father said that he had had his turn later on when he was alone at home. Daniel seemed better on Sunday, and he was so active, kicking and fighting, that they had had to sedate him. He had slept all the next day, and on the following day his lines could go back in. Mother had felt quite desperate when he could not be fed. Father had worked out the equipment and kept an eye on it. Sometimes he was not happy with a particular nurse—one was rather rough. Mother said that she did not mind that so much. I said that I thought he felt that his feelings were being treated roughly.

This dramatic illness seemed to have made the parents feel much closer to Daniel. Mother felt that the twins knew when they were present. She said that Daniel always did something to greet her—for instance, peeing. She told them everything—for instance, where the other one was. At night, when she left them, she said to "Lucy", her daughter: "Now, Lucy, you are in charge." Father looked slightly amazed at all of this. He said that he felt much closer to the twins now, they really were little people to him. He had thought that Daniel was going to die, and mother then agreed that she had thought so too. She said that on that day she had not been able to imagine him in the future, and it had been terrible. They commented that Lucy looked serious all the time, but that this sometimes lifted if they talked to her; Lucy seemed to go deeply into herself. I then went to spend some time with the twins on the unit.

It was in the hot nursery that I went to observe Daniel.

He was lying on his platform naked, on his back, his ventilator strapped to his mouth, his head turned to the right. His skin was very red and paper-thin. He seemed so tiny and vulnerable; I learnt afterwards that he weighed 600 grams. The ultra-violet lamp was shining down on him. He had goggles made of material over his eyes to protect them from the light. He had leads and heavy tubes strapped to his arms and legs. Heavy breathing rippled through his diaphragm. I watched him for 25 minutes as he flexed, stretched, jerked, mouthed, and sucked the ventilator.

Then I went to the next platform, to see his sister, Lucy. I observed the following:

Lucy has a less hot bright lamp shining on her, and her goggles have slipped down from her eyes. There is pressure on her nose and a tube in her mouth. Her hands are free. She has a lead, which is not heavy, stuck to her arm and leads to her legs, but her toes are free. Like her brother, she is very tiny, and her skin looks very dry and thin. Her right arm lies down her side; her fingers curl and then splay open, touching the lead. Her left arm goes up, her hand slightly curls over. Her legs bend up. Her right leg slews across her body to the left. I am filled with awe as I watch her. She becomes very still and seems to go into a deep sleep. Her left toes wriggle slightly. Again she is very still, and she has a frown, seemingly of great concentration. Her mouth closes and opens and stays open. Her right hand moves slowly far out to the right. It is a gentle, graceful movement. Then her left knee moves up so that it is very bent. The nurse comes to check the tubes. Lucy hardly moves. Then her left arm stretches out to the left, very gracefully, and her right to the right. Both arms are stretched out at shoulder level. She looks very abandoned.

I was surprised to see her so lacking in anxiety and enjoying her own body. What amazed me was the beauty of her movements, their grace and delicacy. She was so abandoned and at peace, the vulnerability was almost unbearable. As she stretched out with such delicious pleasure, I remembered her mother telling me that the twins came early because there was no more room inside her—they were too cramped.

At this point the nurse put an antibiotic through a tube in Lucy's foot:

Lucy squirms a little and grimaces. It feels like a mild protest. The nurse says that she is a bad colour, like a black baby. Suddenly Lucy gives a little cry. The nurse rather roughly pulls the goggles over her eyes. She squirms a bit and then is still, but not peaceful as she was.

The charm was broken. I think there was something here that the nurse could not bear to see. She made her provocative remark and pulled the goggles over Lucy's eyes. Then a doctor came and turned the lamp off. She had to take blood from Lucy to test her oxygen levels—a thing that has to be done several times a day and which the babies soon learn to expect and dread.

Lucy is squirming, her left leg is thrashing up, and she arches her back. The doctor puts a different light on in order to see what she is doing. She is standing beside Lucy, putting on her gloves. The doctor says that at any moment she can be called to the labour ward. She feels like a mother with ten children, she can be called at any time and is always being interrupted. She remembers one job where someone followed her into the toilet and went on talking to her while she was in there. Lucy is crying and squirming but is not desperate. The doctor's bleep goes off, and she hurries away. Lucy is still. She squirms and cries a little in a rather pathetic way, moving her shoulders and squirming her trunk. She arches her back and goes red all over. Her left arm stretches high up. The nurse comes back and asks rather crossly where the doctor is, and I say that I think she has gone to the labour ward. She turns the light off and the lamp back on. Lucy stretches her arms and legs very wide, she yawns and whimpers. Her right hand goes down and touches her right knee, and she is quiet. She opens her mouth, but I cannot hear a cry. She dribbles a lot of bubbles and then stretches. She arches her back off the bed and cries. Her left leg stretches far out and then up and she cries again.

The space around Lucy, which had seemed so sensuously spacious, then felt like a nightmarish vacuum. The doctor was feeling persecuted, unable to attend to any job without the risk of interruption, low on resources, and with no privacy to deal with any of her bad experiences. Lucy was in a similar position. She, too, was vulnerable to any interruption. She seemed to try to scrape the bad experience off her, and in going red and straining perhaps she was trying to evacuate it. Her arching and squirming also seemed to be attempts to avoid something persecuting. Perhaps she was trying to "bubble" this persecutor out of her. Her capacity to regulate herself was remarkable. As I noticed how strong my reactions to her were, I thought that her ability to evoke interest and admiration, and her sense of agency, augured well for her. But at this moment she had to bear the brunt of the nurse's bad temper, then was dismayed by the approach of the doctor, knowing already that this might involve pain; but the pain did not come because the doctor was called away. How could she begin to make sense of this unpredictable world? She touched her right knee with her right hand: a little comfort, a little connection. But she could not hold this for long, and with her dribbling, arching, and crying she seemed to succumb to feelings of persecution.

When the twins were 10 days old, I learned at the psychosocial meeting that Daniel had chronic lung disease and a small cyst on the brain. Nobody knew how serious this might be. Lucy was doing very well: she was now on a prong, a less radical form of ventilation. That day I watched Daniel. He had been through a crisis.

> Daniel has a ventilator to his mouth. He is wearing a vest and looks more comfortable. He is lying on his back. His feet are free of bandaging, and his legs are straight. His right arm is out to the side. His left arm bends up; this hand has heavy bandaging around the palm. His eyes are closed. He is very still and is breathing gently. His eyes move under his lids as if they would open, but they don't. He mouths the plastic of the ventilator. His right fingers move very slightly. His head moves very slightly. His right fingers open, and he mouths slightly. His fingers move, and his thumb goes to his forefinger. His tongue goes out to the plastic. He moves his head, his hands, his feet, and then rests. And then he is very still. The nurse says that he is comfortable now, his chest drain is out, that it must have hurt him. He moves his feet slightly, mouths, and then his feet jerk. He stops moving and is very still. I notice that when he is still, I find it difficult to imagine his experience. He stretches in rather a sensual way. His feet jerk, and he stretches.

As I watched, I thought I could see a kind of dance emerging—or was it a conversation? It was very tentative, but one part of Daniel's body moved and another part seemed to answer. Forefinger came to thumb, tongue to plastic. Perhaps he was making some connections. And the nurse was able to think about his experience. I moved on to Lucy.

> She has a frown, and her face is rather crumpled around the prong that goes into her nose. She is lying on her tummy, and she is now wearing a vest. She is facing to the right; her right arm is down, and her left arm is up. A blanket covers her to her waist. Her left hand flexes. She opens her mouth, and I do not know whether it is to yawn or to cry. She closes her mouth, then opens it and leaves it slackly open. Her left fingers move, and her mouth moves around the tubes. Her left fingers move again, and then she is very still. She gives a shuddery breath. Her mouth moves on the tubes. Her eyebrows flicker. Her eyelids try to open but do not succeed. Her eyebrows go up again

and again. She is mouthing. Her mouth draws back very slightly, and she repeats this. She jerks. She moves her right hand, and her breathing becomes more laboured. She is very still. The knuckles of her right hand move against the sheet, and she stretches out her thumb. Her mouth moves, and there follows a very slight movement of her right hand. There is a little mouthing. Her eyebrows rise, and her eyes open very briefly. They close, open, close, and she is still. Her right hand moves. Her eyelids go up, and her eyes open. I am stunned by their blue. The fingers of her right hand splay open, close, open, and then rest down against the sheet. Lucy opens her eyes and looks around. She closes them. She splays open her fingers and seems to nestle back into herself. Her right eye opens, then both, and then they close. They open again. I wish that her mother were here to greet her.

I thought that Lucy was making a connection between her mouth and her right hand—particularly her thumb. Again I was stunned by her beauty, particularly when she opened her eyes and I saw their blue. I felt that she was in some kind of transitional space—opening out to the world and closing back into herself—outwards and backwards. She opened her eyes to see what was out there and nestled back into herself. This was very serious work for Lucy, and I wished that she had her mother's recognition and support at that moment. As I wondered about this transitional space, I thought of the great beauty of those architectural transitional spaces, the balconies and loggias of Renaissance Italy, and of the kind of excitement they can inspire. This, I think, is connected to a sense of expectancy: one stands on the balcony longing to see the approach of the loved one. This seemed to be a moment of such hope for Lucy.

When the twins were 2 weeks old, I met the Smith parents again, this time on the unit. Mrs Smith was having problems about her room on the postnatal ward, which was needed for another woman whose baby had died. A compromise was suggested: Mrs Smith should have it for one more night and then be given a room in the Nurses' Home. She said that she had not minded giving up her room to this woman, although the woman had eventually decided to go home. What she minded was that they had told her in the morning that she had to move out, and she knew that Daniel was going to have his prong put back in, and she had wanted to come down and sort him out. The nurses had said that she could do that, but they might pack her things up while she was with him. She had not wanted them to do that because some of her things were very personal. So she packed them away herself, and when she got downstairs, the doctor was already working on Daniel. She felt that the nurses could not give her that hour, and she was very upset with them. She repeated this many times.

The parents went on to talk about the weekend, which, they said, had been bad. Father was worried about there not being enough staff; he wondered what would happen if all the babies went into crisis at once. A very sick baby had been admitted, and everyone seemed to be working on it, even the nurse who should have been looking after the twins. He went on to say that it really was not safe on the unit with so few nurses—that Lucy had stopped breathing and mother had stimulated her and got her breathing again, but he wondered what would have happened if they had not been there. Father said that he wanted to be reasonable, but he also wanted the best care for the babies. He repeated that he liked it here on the unit; in a funny way it felt like home. It was a relief from outside, where no one really understood what they were going through. He felt quite snappy at work. He talked about wanting to slap someone's face. I said that perhaps it was rather surprising to him to be having murderous feelings. He looked very shocked and denied that they were murderous. But mother interrupted and agreed with me that they were murderous. She said that she had had very nasty feelings about the woman whose baby had died. She had thought that the nurses should have helped her because she had live babies. We made another appointment, but they went on talking. Mother told me of people's comments about what she must have done to bring on the birth prematurely, and her anger and guilt about that.

It seemed that both parents were finding it hard to find a space to bear all they were going through. Mother needed her own room, which could be personal. Father felt helped by the unit, but his workplace provided somewhere safer to express his anger. They were both overloaded with emotional work and had very little privacy to get on with it. Although father found it hard to leave the unit, this did give him some freedom, whereas mother was stuck on the unit and perhaps felt more in danger of claustrophobia. The unit seemed like a good place, but sometimes the resources were not adequate. There was some reality to this. The unit was clearly understaffed—any observant parent could see this. Additionally, they had a worry about their own capacity to deal with so much anxiety and uncertainty. Also the impact of having twins was hitting them, adding to their anxiety about resources.

When I went to see Lucy on her 23rd day, she was wearing a babygro, looking comfortable and compact, lying on her tummy. She swivelled her feet on her toes and lifted her bottom off the ground, getting some purchase with her feet. She was grasping the collar of her suit with her right hand. She let go of it and grasped it again and again. Perhaps she was testing to see what was out there to come up against—what was there to hold on to.

I spoke to the parents that same day. They told me that Daniel was doing much better, but that Lucy was stuck on her oxygen. Whereas she had always seemed the fitter baby, she now seemed to have fallen behind her brother. We talked more about the impact of having and being twins. They said they worried about whether the babies missed each other and planned to hold them together. Mother had left the nurses' rooms and gone home but was coming in every day to be with the twins, and father joined her on the unit in the evening after work. Mother said that she was ready to go home: she trusted the twins to look after themselves. She felt that Daniel was more content with life, that Lucy pushed herself too hard. They were disturbed because another baby had been moved through to the cool nursery and that baby's mother was upset at the change, although this was a step forward. They were adamant that the twins must always be together. Father expressed worry about whether they would be moved back to their local hospital.

Mother, with her placid manner, seemed to deny a lot of anxiety. Perhaps this enabled her to function. Some of her distress may have been split off into the mother who was upset by her baby's move to the cool nursery.

The next day I went to see Daniel. He was on his back, looking to the right.

His right leg is stretched out to the side. His left leg is crossed. His right arm is down, touching a lead of the equipment. His left hand is grasping his cotton top. His eyes are open, and he is looking around. His right foot moves against the lead. . . . He looks around. His left hand opens and closes. His right hand opens and closes. His thumb goes to his forefinger. His mouth opens, and his right hand moves towards it. His eyes open more, and his hand moves nearer to his mouth. He looks around and seems to be searching for something with his mouth. Mouthing. . . . Both hands are in loose fists. He opens his eyes and squirms a little. His eyes close, and he seems to have gone to sleep. He is quiet. . . . His mouth opens, and then he opens his eyes. He looks and looks as if trying to focus. He jerks and then frowns.

I thought Daniel was looking for something outside, trying to make some connection. I wondered if he had given up the attempt and sunk back into himself. When he woke up again, he seemed to have lost his focus, perhaps to have lost the idea of searching for something.

At the psychosocial meeting that week it was confirmed that Daniel was doing better than Lucy, that she was still stuck on her oxygen requirement. There was concern that mother was becoming ground down by Lucy's lack of progress. That weekend Daniel had another crisis and was moved to the other side of the nursery to be nearer to an oxygen outlet. The parents were upset that the twins were no longer placed side by side. As I looked at Lucy, a nurse asked me if I had seen the parents recently. She felt that they were not so together as they had been. I pointed out that this might have to do with the twins not being so together, and she agreed. It seemed to me that there are problems in thinking about twins. It is very hard to think about one of them except in terms of the other, and then questions arise as to whether they are two separate beings or two halves of one being.

I went to see Mrs Smith. She told me that the twins had been separated. She thought that Daniel missed Lucy, that he was rather like her husband. She had always thought that. Daniel cried sometimes—he just seemed to be unhappy. If she stroked him and

talked to him, he calmed down. She went on to say that she preferred it when Lucy was unwell; but that her husband preferred it
when Daniel was. She said that she had felt helped by me to
question things; for instance, there had been a problem about the
headbox—she had found a larger one and had cleaned it. She felt
that it was important to be able to see through it, that it could seem
like a barrier. Sometimes she let the side of the incubator down.
She felt more confident to do these things but not in control—
perhaps she would never feel in control again.

I believed that mother's thoughts about the twins being separated must in part be linked with her own depression about being
separated from her babies, both by birth and then by the hospital
context. She had told me that she trusted them to look after themselves, and at first she had left Lucy in charge. It seemed that she
had fantasies that they could look after each other, and perhaps
Lucy, with whom she identified, carried some of her maternal
function, so that mother could bear to leave them. In saying that
she preferred Lucy to be the one who was unwell, she was perhaps
handing on to Lucy some harshness that she herself felt in her
deprived maternal state. Lucy then had to manage on very little,
just as she did. Perhaps Daniel, too, was thought of as much more
in danger and was identified with mother's dead brother. There
remained the issue of the small cyst on his brain, and what this
might mean. It certainly seemed that Daniel evoked in his mother
a powerful protectiveness, which perhaps she felt that Lucy did
not need.

I went to watch Lucy. She seemed to be concentrating very
hard on bringing her hand to her mouth. She brought her thumb to
her forehead and then away, and then back, all the time mouthing.
Her mouth was searching. Her eyes, too, were searching. Lucy
went on doing this with great attention. She brought her hand to
her open mouth and smiled. I was very absorbed in her work.
Then the doctor came to take blood. She apologized to Lucy as she
did so. When it was over, Lucy put her hand right up against her
nose; her eyes were closed, and she was very still. Later her eyes
opened, but they were no longer focused. She looked red and
bloated. Her hand came near her face, her eyes opened, and her
hands moved rather shakily. She was less sure of her movements.
She had been assaulted and arrested in her purposeful activity. I

think she had been involved in a very intelligent effort to make sense of her world, and this had been interrupted.

When I went to see Daniel, he, too, was upset:

> He is on his back in the headbox, with his arms outside the box. A tube leads into his mouth. He is flailing around with his arms and legs. His face is wrinkled up. There are lots of bubbles around the oxygen tube. The nurse is going to suction him out. His face is screwed up. His mouth is open. His left leg goes out straight. He opens his mouth wider as she starts to poke into his mouth with the suction equipment. His crying goes on and on, loudly, and I notice that I have stopped watching. The nurse interrupts the suctioning and puts his right hand into the headbox. He tries to pull out his tubes with his right hand. She takes this hand out of the headbox. Now his left hand is inside the headbox, bent up behind his head. His right hand flails around outside the box, and he is crying. After a while the nurse tries to make him more comfortable. He brings his left hand round to his mouth and holds it there, jammed against the box. His right hand is lying open, palm upwards.

The suctioning here felt so invasive that I found it very hard to watch. Daniel seemed to want to get rid of the persecutor, to pull out the tubes. The headbox seemed to be an additional impediment to connection. He could not get his active right hand to his mouth. It seemed that what could be a comfort to him, his right hand, he could not get to, and what was available to him was not what he wanted. Perhaps the headbox also acted as a barrier to the nurse's empathy for him. Finally she tried to make him more comfortable and his right hand lay palm upwards as if in a gesture of resignation.

A few days later I watched him when he was lying quietly. He was on his back, with his head in the headbox. He repeatedly held his thumb to his forefinger. Opening his eyes seemed to be connected to opening his mouth:

> Daniel's mouth opens and closes on the tube. His eyes open and close. His mouth opens and closes. Eyes open slightly. Left leg stretches out. His left hand goes down straight and then

bends up. . . . His left thumb goes to his forefinger. His eyes open. He stretches. His left hand lifts so that his arm is against the corner of the headbox. . . . His right hand is in a fist with the thumb to forefinger. His mouth opens wide. His left hand opens a little. He stretches with his eyes open. His left hand goes down straight, then moves so that his forefinger touches his knee. That hand then stretches up inside the headbox, and then goes down straight out of the headbox. . . Daniel's mouth moves. His hand is loosely held with the thumb against his two first fingers. His hand moves. His thumb is now against the forefinger, then between the first and second finger. His hand then opens with its back against the sheet. His fist stretches out, and he is sucking. . . His thumb settles against his forefinger. His hand moves down and then up and right down. All the time the thumb is touching the forefinger.

I thought that perhaps this pair—the thumb and the forefinger—go exploring together, trying to make sense of the world.

I saw the Smiths in the fifth week after the twins' birth. Mr Smith, coming in a few minutes after his wife, said that Daniel had just had a bradycardia when I walked in, and that this had happened the week before as well. He repeated this several times. I wondered if I was supposed to be the repository of a whole range of chaotic feelings that were hard to sort out: blame that I did not know about this, guilt that I had walked into the nursery and caused such a thing to occur, anger that I should be accused of such a thing, and mindlessness that a world of such primitive superstition should rule. Lucy's heart had been examined by a Brompton heart specialist that day. Mother had not told father that it was happening because he "might have had a heart attack". Mother said quite gaily that it was all right, except that the specialist had had cold hands and Lucy had not liked this. It seemed to me that there were lethal amounts of anxiety around, and there was a serious question about who could bear it. Father went on to express his tremendous sense of guilt: guilt about his work, guilt about the twins. They talked about the impact of twins—always having to choose one, always having to make one wait; that whenever you are with one, you are not with the other. Father talked about how much he liked the unit—it felt like home; they even had a good laugh with the unit staff in the evenings. It seemed that the unit provided some kind of holding situation for him. When I asked mother about herself, she said that on that day, as she was driving in, she suddenly had a lump in her throat. She thought there were a lot of feelings there. I thought that she had stifled them, and that perhaps this was the only way that she could function in a situation that was so cruel to her maternal feelings. I thought she had some identification with the cold-handed surgeon, perhaps unconsciously thinking that he could not do what he had to do unless his feelings were kept cold and detached. People who were more in touch, like her husband, might have a heart attack.

Mother's defensive attitude began to have repercussions on the unit. The nurses felt that she was not very maternal. In fact, she was a very faithful and involved mother, which can sometimes make the nurses feel unnecessary, or jealous, or even guilty that they cannot do more. This mother also kept very close control of her feelings, not presenting herself as needy. But perhaps the nurses were responding to the difference in her relationship to her son and her daughter. She poured tenderness on to Daniel, who, she felt, was more needy, and she seemed to feel that Lucy could manage on her own more. It is possible that Lucy, with her powerful capacity to feel, express, and evoke feelings, was quite difficult for her mother when she was finding it so necessary to suppress her own feelings.

I noticed that Lucy had become very adept at getting her hand into her mouth and sucking on it.

She holds her right hand in a fist at the back of her neck, her left hand to her mouth. This left hand is on a voyage of discovery. Her fingers flex out and go into a fist, which she sucks on, and then she puts her little finger into her mouth. Her hand then curls over her mouth, and she sucks strongly and rhythmically. Her forefinger goes to her cheek, and her fingers stretch and curl. Her right hand answers, opening and closing. Her left hand curls back over her mouth. This dance or conversation goes on with evident delight. She sucks more vigorously and stretches deliciously. Her eyes open; her forefinger points up, almost touching her eye. Her other fingers curl over her mouth.

> She is sucking and looking around. Her eyes close. Her fingers move down to her nose and then form a very loose fist over her mouth. Her eyes are opening and closing. Her fingers stretch up. Her two forefingers stretch up towards her eye, touching her cheek. She yawns. Her fingers splay out, stretching. Her hand leaves her mouth, which is opening and closing, and goes out against the headbox. This left hand comes back and curls loosely over her nose.

She seemed to be enumerating important zones with her hand—they are her mouth, her eyes, and her nose—and then she reaches out to touch the limits of her world, the headbox, and back. In Bion's terms, she had a preconception and seemed to be looking for a realization (Bion, 1962). She appeared very contained, very intent and able to bear frustration.

When I saw her five days later, she was being fed every two hours nasogastrically.

> Now she is searching with her mouth. Her mouth gets stuck on the opening to the headbox, her right hand is outside the box with one finger against it. This hand then bangs out against the side of the cot. As I watch her, I long to pick her up. Her mouth opens, and her tongue moves in and out. She is sucking, and her right thumb moves. Her mouth is searching. This goes on. She tries to be content with her tongue movements in and out. Her hands are both outside the headbox, and again she thumps her right hand against the side of the cot. The nurse moves her up into the headbox so that she is not squashed down and puts her left arm inside. Her eyes open and close, open and close, her tongue goes out, her left arm stretches out of the headbox: Her eyes open and close, moving around but not particularly looking around, more as if her eyelids are like curtains.

I felt that Lucy had an idea of needing something, that she banged on the cot trying to get a response, but she did not get it and withdrew. I came to think that she was discouraged, and, thinking back, I felt that she had been looking for a response for some time, that this had been crystallized in her attempt to delineate different zones, and that she was suffering from a lack of reply.

At the same time Daniel was getting the reputation on the unit of being a very cross baby. He would not wait for feeds. He was out of his headbox and was making his will felt. I think that mother enjoyed this assertiveness and perhaps felt reassured by it. She was now putting him to the breast. Father had picked him up that morning, and after he had put him down, he would not settle. His anger and inability to bear frustration seemed to have galvanized everyone, whereas Lucy was sinking into the background.

That evening at our weekly meeting mother appeared in an angry mood too. She asked why she had not been told to rest more when she was pregnant. She could have stopped working so hard. She said that she felt very up and down. She and her husband needed practical help. She felt let down by the family. People wanted the glamorous bits—not the washing and shopping. It was so hard getting everything done. Father came in, repeating the same things. I said that I thought they felt very isolated from family and friends. They agreed and said that nobody understood. Mother went on to say that Daniel had been very angry and had had an infection over the weekend. She had put him to the breast twice, and he had liked it. Lucy was much slower. Mother said that she sometimes worried about whether there was something wrong with her. When she was at home on her own, she would worry about whether Lucy was all right or whether the doctors had missed something. I wondered whether she was unconsciously worried about the split she had made between Daniel and Lucy. She encouraged Daniel's lusty demand for service, life, satisfaction by answering him, whereas Lucy, perhaps the more psychologically strong and at first the more physically strong, was the bearer of strong emotion and now was made to carry the frustration and depression. Daniel, and not Lucy, had been put to the breast, which I felt Lucy had been looking for so heartrendingly for days.

The issue was discussed of the twins being moved back to their local hospital. The parents did not want this. I wondered whether unconsciously they were holding back Lucy, the stronger baby, so that they could not be transferred yet.

In the 8th week Lucy appeared to have lost her focus. She seemed to have lost her delicacy and her movements had become grosser and less informed by intentionality. She seemed to feel persecuted, trying to get rid of something—sneezing, hiccoughing, crying, mouthing, flailing her arms:

> Her hand goes towards her mouth but does not touch it. The nurse thinks that she does not like the headbox. Both hands go out to the side as if she is trying to gain a purchase. She stares at the oxygen outlet; her right hand stretches up and pushes the oxygen outlet to her mouth, and her mouth opens against it again, and again and she is crying. She pants hard and quietens. Her right hand is crooked around the oxygen tube. Again her head lifts, searching, and she is crying. And again her mouth jams up against the oxygen tube. She moves away and she is panting. This desperate search continues. Her eyes open and close, she looks around and seems unfocused.

It seemed as if she was making a huge attempt to gain a purchase, to pull herself out of a persecuted state, and to find something. This was full of pain for her and heartbreaking to watch. Eventually she took refuge in dismantling her perceptions, and she became unfocused. I often spoke to mother on the ward, and at around this time I noticed that she did not speak about Lucy unless I did.

At the psychosocial meeting I found that others besides me were worried by mother's seeming lack of attachment to Lucy. It was decided to put Lucy on a trickle of oxygen from a small tube taped to her nose, so that she could be taken out of the headbox and the parents could lift her out of her cot more easily.

In the ninth week I went to the cool nursery with these thoughts in my head. There I found Mrs Smith with Lucy.

> Mother was changing Lucy's cardigan. She was worried about whether the new cardigan was too rough. Lucy was wide awake, looking around and at her mother. Mother kept on saying that she was going to pick her up for a little cuddle. I felt anxious about whether she was really going to do this. Eventually mother did pick her up, and I helped with the leads. She sat down, and I asked her if I could stay to watch. She said that I could. Lucy was nestled in her left arm, looking up into her mother's eyes. She looked content but was also looking for

something with her mouth. Her mother said that she had not got a very good suck, the speech therapist would try to help her with it. I said that I thought she loved her mother holding her and that she was looking for something to go into her mouth. Mother looked interested. She dipped her little finger into some sterilized water and put it into Lucy's mouth. Lucy took it and sucked strongly. She rested every now and then, but her suck was strong and rhythmic. Mother said that Lucy was sucking her finger far in; mother was afraid of hurting her throat; and that every now and then Lucy shot mother's finger out. I said that I thought she liked being in control. Mother laughed and said, "Just like her mother . . . or so her father thinks." Mother was laughing and smiling. I had never seen her look so animated. She was obviously thrilled. She pointed out to me that Lucy was holding her mother's hand to her mouth. Her little fingernails were in her mother's hand. If mother relaxed her hand, Lucy held it there. Lucy looked unbelievably well and right. This continued for some time.

Then it was time for Lucy's feed. Mother said that she would put Lucy down and put the milk down the tube. I said that if she wanted to go on holding Lucy, I could hold the tube, and she agreed. In the meantime Daniel's feed was forgotten. A passing nurse suggested that mother put Lucy to the breast. Mother seemed hesitant. Lucy went on sucking on her finger. The nurse suggested it again. Mother looked around nervously and asked if there were any midwives around. She undid her shirt and put Lucy near her nipple. Lucy put her tongue against it, opened her mouth to take it, sucked, and then cried. This happened several times, with Lucy quite clearly going for the breast and then coming off it. Mother felt that she was too hungry, that she needed feeding. She did her shirt up, and another nurse suggested a bottle. Mother tried the bottle. Lucy licked it, took it, rested, took it, rested, looked sleepy. After some while mother decided to put the rest down the tube. I held the tube and suggested to mother that she put her finger into Lucy's mouth, so that she associated sucking with the feeling in her tummy. She did this, and Lucy began sucking vigorously. I suggested that she tried the bottle which had just a little bit of milk left in it. Mother checked with the nurse, who agreed. Lucy resisted the bottle, turning her head. She screwed up her face and then, with her head turned away from mother, took the bottle in very good strong sucks. She held her right hand inside mother's shirt, and mother said that she was stroking her breast. The milk down the tube was finished. Very little was left in the bottle, and Lucy seemed to have finished. But mother wanted this tiny amount put down the tube. I remembered how, when the twins were just born and mother was expressing tiny amounts of milk, a nurse had said to her it did not matter how small it was, it was so precious and could be put down the tube, and mother had felt that this was the one thing that only she could do for her babies.

Lucy lay back on mother's lap, very relaxed. One eye had stayed open during the bottle feed. Now both were closed. Mother asked me why I had particularly sat with her this afternoon, and whether I had thought that Lucy was neglected. I said that I had thought that Lucy had lost her focus. She had wanted to suck, and I thought that she had become confused about it. She agreed and said that she had thought that too. She noted that Lucy's breathing was easy now, not laboured, although she was on her back. She thought that Lucy would improve now that she was out of her headbox. She touched her chest very gently and watched her breathing. She looked at her baby daughter with tremendous pleasure and delight, talking to her, smiling and hugging her. She said that now they would show the doctors, and Lucy would soon be off her oxygen. This echoed my suspicion that Lucy was hanging on to the oxygen in some depressed state, unable to find anything else to hold on to. I felt that mother and baby had found each other.

Five days later Mrs Smith was holding Lucy up against her shoulder. She said that she had had her at the breast, and when she had taken her off, Lucy had sat with both hands in fists, almost quivering with excitement. She was going to try to breast-feed Daniel with help from the breast-feeding counsellor. She was having coffee, and it was past Daniel's feeding time. Again I was surprised by mother's lack of a sense of urgency.

When we got to Daniel, the SHO was trying to take blood from Daniel's right hand. He was writhing in his cot. Everything seemed to be in disarray. He was screaming, and the SHO was finding it hard to bear, having been up all night. Whenever she rested, he calmed down. Mother and the breast-feeding coun-sellor were talking to Lucy a couple of feet away. I wondered why mother did not come to comfort him. I talked to him as he looked around. Mother turned round and remarked that I was observing him. I said something rather feeble. When the doctor finished, mother came to him. She said that soon she would give him a cuddle. He was looking at her. She tutted because there was some blood on one sleeve. His other arm was out of his suit. She wondered how she would be able to dress him with all this equipment on his arm. She got him a vest and started to change him. He was watching her. She thought that his nappy needed to be changed. She was taking so long that I was feeling desperate. She could not find the baby bath, which turned out to be a kind of ointment. Daniel was in a mess, so she cleaned him up. She said they were very short staffed and that he had not been changed. She looked up in the book to see when he had been changed—she misread it and then checked again. She repeated that they were very short-staffed but re-marked that even so it depended on which nurse was on whether the baby would get looked after.

At the beginning of this observation I felt desperate but then even more frantic at mother's slow, methodical manner. I wondered whether mother's being more in touch with Lucy had made her less in touch with Daniel. If this were the case, what had I done to this little boy, by helping his mother to be more in touch with his sister? I felt an atmosphere of blame and negligence.

All this time mother was cleaning Daniel, and he was watching her and crying. She told him that she would give him a cuddle in a minute. Then the nurse came to put eye-drops in his eyes for a test due that afternoon to see if he had any blindness. She tried his left eye, and he closed it tightly, screaming. She tried to prize it open. He opened it a slit, and she put the drops in, most of them running out. Then she tried the other eye. Again it was tightly shut, and he was screaming. The nurse asked mother to help. She said that she would do his nappy up and then wash her hands. While she was away, he relaxed, and I said to the nurse to do it quickly, which she did. He was crying and blinking, and I wondered if it stung.

It did seem in this observation as if there was a terrible attack on seeing and also on insight. Daniel's mother seemed to find it unbearable to see him in such a bad state, so she undermined her insight into his state of mind. As I watched the drama unfold, I felt full of a dreadful urgency and had a searing headache for the rest of the day. Daniel had stared into his mother's eyes, feeling perhaps that he was making little impact with his screaming, and perhaps he then felt attacked by these drops forced into his eyes. Over all this hung the dreadful, but unacknowledged, prospect of the eye test that afternoon, to see whether Daniel had any retinal damage, an iatrogenic hazard of prematurity.

The following day Lucy was waiting for her midday feed. She still had a tube in her mouth for nasogastric feeding, but in this observation she seemed full of gentle hope for the breast.

Both hands are in front of her in gentle fists. She is still. Both her hands go to her mouth and then away from her mouth and then splay out in front of her mouth. Her hands are touching each other. Her eyebrows go up, and her eyelids flutter. Her eyes open for a second. Her hands move together. Her head is moving around. Her eyelids flutter. Her right finger tips move on her left wrist. She makes very little sucking movements. Her eyebrows go up. Her mouth opens. Her tongue goes in and out. Her left hand goes into a tighter fist. Her right-hand fingers are still lightly on her wrist. Suddenly she jerks, as if she is hurt in her mouth. Then she is still. Her eyes open and close. Her right hand holds on to her left cardigan sleeve. She is rooting around with her head, stretching out her hands. Her mouth opens, and her tongue comes out.

This seems to be an evocation of being at the breast, of licking, sucking, caressing with her fingertips. This state seems to be threatened by some frustration, some disappointment, some pain, but this is borne. She holds on and the hope lives.

A few days later mother arrived at Daniel's feeding time. She said that she would quickly put the milk down the tube. I suggested to her that she breast-fed him, to which she agreed. At that moment Dr "Carter", the consultant, arrived to talk to her. I pointed out that it was a matter of who should wait, the baby or the consultant. He argued that he could not get to see any of the mothers because they were all feeding their babies, and I pointed out that it was a baby unit. However, Daniel lost. The consultant then informed the mother that the twins were to be transferred to their local hospital after the weekend. She told me later that she felt that they had only been moved because the unit was so full; that she had felt dumped. I thought that this was another premature event, without enough time for thought and assimilation. She rang her husband. Daniel was still waiting to be fed. She said that she would tube-feed him, no, bottle, it was too late for the breast. Daniel came towards her breast and then took the bottle, sucking quite strongly. Meanwhile it was time for Lucy's feed, and mother told the nurse to put it down the tube. Very quickly mother felt that Daniel was tired and should have the rest down the tube. I think this was the end of a real attempt to breast-feed Lucy. I think that mother felt dropped, perhaps used in an institutionalized way, and she then treated her children in a similar way in this observation.

The twins moved to their local hospital fairly uneventfully. The parents came to feel that it was a step forward: they had their own little room, and this unit was less hi-tech. They said that they missed me and one or two other members of staff. Mother said that Lucy complained more than Daniel, that she was a more difficult baby. I thought that Lucy represented the unbearable feelings surrounding the prematurity and experience on the NICU and was then felt to be problematic.

This view remained with me when I visited the twins in hospital and then at home. Mother regularly breast-fed Daniel, but only occasionally fed Lucy "for comfort". She would make Lucy wait for her feed while she fed Daniel, even when Lucy was due first. Lucy had become stuck on a small level of oxygen, which delayed the discharge home. Mother was angry about this, because Daniel was ready to go home, and she felt that he was getting bored in hospital and that Lucy was holding him back.

Once the twins returned home at just over 3 months, paternal grandmother came to stay during the week for the first two months. Lucy slept in the same room as grandmother. Daniel slept with his parents, so that mother could put him to the breast as soon as he woke up. It was mostly grandmother who fed Lucy, although mother admitted that Lucy fed much better when she fed her herself. I found these visits quite painful. Mother always talked about Daniel, and even when I asked about Lucy, she would draw the conversation back to him. Mother seemed to want me to visit but was rather distant.

Then on the first visit after grandmother had gone home, mother greeted me warmly:

> The twins had had their potato and were sitting in their little chairs in the living-room. Mother picked up Daniel and gave him his bottle. Lucy looked round the room, banged her legs, and looked at the television. Mother said that I could pick her up. I did, and she sat on my lap, looking around. I held her so that she could see her mother, which seemed to be what she wanted, and she turned and gave me an enormous smile. Daniel continued to feed, and every so often Lucy would become disturbed. Mother thought that she had a little colic, so I put her over my shoulder and patted her back. Mother did the same to Daniel, and he gradually fell asleep against her. Lucy put her mouth right in against my neck, where she found some bare skin and began sucking, with both her hands held up in fists against me. This reminded me very vividly of her in hospital. Every now and then she would lift her head and put it from one side to the other. Mother told me that they were only just coming out of a state of shock and getting their feelings back. She seemed much more alive and friendly than she had been on previous visits. One bad thing, she said, was that they had fallen out with her husband's mother. There had been lots of bad feeling between them. Grandmother had mostly taken over the care of Lucy. She was not very motherly and had not fed

Lucy well and Lucy was doing much better now that grand-mother had gone.

Mother said that Lucy was feeding better, and that both babies now slept together in the nursery, so there was no preferential treatment for Daniel, although sometimes in the morning they crawled in to get Daniel so that Lucy would not see them. So long as she did not see them, she did not make a fuss. Mother said that she hoped I did not mind her talking, it was a great relief. As we spoke, Lucy settled right in against my neck and fell deeply asleep. Mother seemed closer to Lucy than before, more loving, as she looked at her in my arms. I wondered whether Lucy fell asleep so comfortably with the relief that her mother's feelings had another home. Mother looked down at Daniel and told me that she was often overwhelmed by waves of love for him, and when she thought how nearly she had lost him, she could hardly bear it.

It seemed that as mother began to recover her feelings, she was able to be closer to Lucy, although her daughter still had to be kept at some distance and was seen as potentially overwhelming—as, I think, mother felt her own feelings might turn out to be. Once mother became closer to Lucy, it was painful for her to acknowl-edge having been apart from her. It seemed that grandmother was blamed for having been a barrier between them, and the bad unmotherly aspects were put into grandmother, hated there, and got rid of. In contrast to the unit's earlier view, the parents seemed to agree that Lucy was more difficult, and mother said that she was more difficult to love. But father said that he was more in-volved with her, she had a greater range of emotions. I thought that he was obviously enchanted by her. Gradually over the next few weeks Lucy became more content and more secure. She was very active, kicking a great deal, but most remarkably she had an ecstatic smile, very intense eyes, and a joyful gurgle. When I vis-ited, I felt that she claimed my eyes and my attention, making it hard for me to look at Daniel. Daniel, the parents said, was the more easygoing baby, but he appeared very serious and very in-volved with his mother. Father said that Daniel had a special smile only for his mother, whereas Lucy's smile was the same for everyone. Father talked about beginning to think back over everything that had happened—doing this at odd moments of the day—and mother agreed that she did this too. It seemed to me that they were now elaborating a wider range of emotions. I wondered whether the more they managed to integrate and digest the experience they had been through, the more they were able to turn to Lucy and enjoy her, and the less she had to represent the difficulties and frustrations they had had to manage.

I left them sitting side by side on the sofa, mother feeding Daniel and father feeding Lucy, proud of their babies and reflecting on their experience, telling me and checking things out with each other. As in our first meeting, I was struck by their ability to listen to each other, to take turns, and to recount their own close observations of their babies.

* * *

So what can we learn from a story like this? First, let us consider the observation of such premature babies: the project of trying to enter and articulate the baby's experience using observation as a tool. The question arises: how do we enter and articulate a baby's experience? Perhaps we do this in part by identification, by drawing on our own infantile experience. But babies like the Smith twins probably activate some of our worst nightmares—to be exposed to such pain and frustration without the mediating protection of a powerful and benign mother. When we observe full-term babies, we usually see mothers bending over their babies, taking in every detail, commenting on it to the baby in a very particular way and thus processing and interpreting his feelings for him. Mother and baby sometimes look at each other with rapt attention. The mother gives meaning to the baby's world, and the baby seems to be looking for meaning. As observers, we enter a situation where meaning is being attributed and built up, and we may add our own construction of what is going on.

The case is rather different with a severely premature baby in an incubator. The mother is necessarily inhibited in her mothering—she cannot pick her baby up, hold him, or feed him. She may be so discouraged by these restrictions that she feels she is not really the mother or that this is not her baby—mothers often say that their baby belongs to the nurses. She may assume that the baby in the incubator cannot hear her; and if he is very premature, his eyes will not be open, so he cannot see her looking at him. Her view of him is obscured by all the equipment, and she may not want to look too carefully because of the pain associated with all that is going on. So the mother's function as the giver of meaning is interfered with. She will probably find it hard to perform her role as the interpreter of her baby's feelings, wishes, and even thoughts as for large amounts of time she will not be present and she is often unable to interpret the world to the baby because it is a world over which she has very little control, a world that she herself may find hard to understand.

So too, I think, it is a hard task for the observer to give meaning to the baby's world. We have to do this in something of a vacuum, aware that the baby is often lacking some essential mediating experience from the mother. At a very crude level the baby is lying in the incubator open to the eyes of anyone, whereas in a normal setting the observer will have to negotiate and win the consent of the mother before we can approach. (Of course, in the hospital setting we have to gain the parents' consent to observe, but the observation is usually of a baby alone, not of a mother-and-baby couple.)

On a more sophisticated level, the baby in the incubator is not having—or if he is, only minimally so—a story woven around him. In baby observations in a baby's home, there is a story that we as observers have to take seriously. Of course, on the unit there is a story in the parents' minds, and there are all kinds of views in the nurses' minds, but what I feel is missing is the minute-by-minute making sense of the world and the baby's own feelings, which begins to construct a world of meaning that can then gradually be available to the baby. So in the NICU we try to imagine, to build up a picture of the baby's experience, but because of the minimized participation of the mother this is a very painful task. We see an experience that is very raw and unmediated. I think that this can lead to two defences. One is to deny the reality of the baby's experience, to claim that it has no meaning, that he is perhaps living in limbo and has yet to enter a world of significance. The other is to construct an elaborate story that may be an adult construction of great imagination. We may be tempted to build on to the baby's experience in a way that is a defence against seeing these tiny babies struggling with a very immature apparatus for understanding. I felt with Lucy and Daniel that their struggle to make sense of their world was hard-fought, very slow, and against a barrage of confusion, and that this confusion had to be borne without the usual mediation. In fact, their mother and father were unusually capable of giving their babies' world meaning, to talk to them, and to offer them a lot of protection, and I think this made a lot of difference to them.

In trying to imagine the baby's experience, we have to reach inside ourselves for any clue of recognition that we can find— hence my thoughts, when I was observing Lucy, about Renaissance architecture. Maybe I thought of this because of the reassuring and orderly calm of these buildings. I think that we use our minds filled with our experience to reach out to the baby, to resonate with it, to meet it. With these babies this is so difficult that we cling to any clue. I find myself casting around for a supervisor who might clarify my experience, partly because the situation of these babies is one that taxes the strength of our own internal objects, but also in a wish for the absent mother to take on the task, which I feel she would be better equipped to undertake than I am. While using our minds as guides in this way, we have to be clear that they are our minds, not the baby's, and that the stories that we construct are our stories, which may or may not be helpful to the baby.

This brings me to my second question: what effect, if any, does the presence of the observer have on the baby and on the parents? Perhaps the effort of the observer to reach out imaginatively to the baby and to bear what is going on, in combination with the parents' efforts in this way, helps the baby to begin to have some notion of its experience being processed. Nurses have commented to me that the babies like my observing them. And babies make it very clear that they are aware when their parents arrive on the unit and start watching and talking to them. In a similar way I think that the observer can be helpful to the parents. The determination of the observer to observe can give the parents more confidence to trust what they see for themselves, to feel more articulate, and to be more powerful in becoming spokespersons for their babies. I think also that being a parent on the unit can be a very lonely experience, and some parents like to talk to someone who is prepared to listen to their fantasies about their babies.

And then, what about the effect of all of this on the staff? To some extent baby observation goes against the psychic defences that tend to be erected on a NICU. The sight of such frail creatures often makes staff withdraw into the protection and impersonality of their medical role. The presence of an observer can help the staff to lay aside this protection. Once they see someone else watching the babies so carefully, they allow themselves to articulate all kinds of ideas about the babies, to talk to them more, and to be more confident in speaking up for them at unit meetings.

At its best, the presence of a child psychotherapist who observes the babies, tries to imagine how the babies are feeling, and is prepared to risk articulating this to the parents and to the staff can improve the atmosphere of a NICU, so that there is not so much denial of the raw and painful experience of the baby. The unit can then offer some of the mediating work that the babies need and can also support the parents in taking on their essential interpretative function for the babies.

CHAPTER FOUR

The issue of respect
in a medical context

The essence of friendship lies . . . in the exercise of a capacity
to perceive, a willingness to respect, and a desire to
understand, the differences between persons.

Richard Wollheim, *The Thread of Life*, 1984

A full-term baby, "Monica", came to the NICU because the doctors were worried by her appearance and floppiness. After extensive investigations it was found that she had a neural migration defect, that her brain had not and could not mature, and she would not live. Monica could not swallow—a nasogastric tube would not stay down—so she received nutrition through a long line. This is a soft, flexible tube that is inserted into a vein and passed to the heart to give the baby all essential nutrients for growth. Her breathing was maintained by a ventilator. The long line had been put in with great difficulty by another hospital, which was in full collaboration with the neonatal unit. Monica's parents were very popular on the unit: their courage and care for their daughter touched the hearts of the unit staff. They listened to the doctors but also voiced their own opinions, and they had good working relations with the nurses.

This seemed to be a tragic situation but one where the parents and staff were in good communication. Monica's condition deteriorated, and the consultant decided with the parents to take her off the ventilator and to allow her parents to hold her while she died. It was thought that she would die within half an hour—or at least quite soon. The nurses cooperated in this. A more private part of the unit was put aside. The consultant was present on the unit and a particular nurse was assigned to them—a person who was sensitive and supportive yet not intrusive. The chaplain came for a short visit. There was a respectful solemnity as people got on with other work.

Monica did not die in half an hour, a day, or a week. The parents moved into a small room in the unit and had Monica with them all the time. They held her, talked to her, and supported each other. She seemed quite relaxed, fading away, although at times she was sick and uncomfortable. Then her long line came out. The question was whether to put it back, which would be very painful for her, or to put in a nasogastric tube, which might make her gag and die in a manner like drowning, or not to feed her at all, but to have her mouth, eyes, and nose kept wet for her comfort. The consultant decided with the parents to do this last, and it was done. He felt he had consulted with the nurses because he had talked to some who were on duty when he came to the decision. But other nurses felt left out of the decision. Their anger seemed to be a mixture of anger at being left out of the making of the decision and anger at the decision made. On the second count their argument was that they were nurses whose job it was to take care of their patients, to fight for their lives, and that not to feed Monica was too dreadful. They said things like "You wouldn't treat a dog like that." They argued with the consultant, and, as the week progressed, he looked more and more worn. Monica lived another five days. During that time the parents came to feel persecuted by the nurses, whose disapproval they sensed. They had not wanted Monica to be given pain killers, but as she became weaker, they agreed to this. When staff went off duty they would call in to see her and were faced by the thought of whether this was the last goodbye. Eventually on a Friday, two and a half weeks after she was taken off the ventilator, Monica died.

* * *

This story illustrates the complex relationships and issues arising on a NICU, and how central the issue of respect is. It is with just such anecdotal illustrations that I hope to delineate more fully the notion of respect.

Much of the time we negotiate the world and the other people in it as so many obstacles in our own path, and it takes some imagination to take full cognisance of other people in their full independent reality. In Kleinian psychoanalytic theory it is thought that the baby gradually becomes aware that it is dependent on its mother, who is an independent person who may go away. As we become older, we are aware of her vulnerability: that she may fall ill or even die. The baby is aware of this only fleetingly, and the impact of this insight is quite terrifying. The baby may well retreat into some kind of omnipotent defence, perhaps thinking that he controls his mother or that there is no danger to her nor, therefore, to him. Sometimes he is able to accept the realization of her otherness and his dependence on her—this is called the depressive position by Kleinians. He may become concerned about his mother's safety, feeling that she is in danger both from the rest of the world and from himself. He becomes afraid that his projections of his feelings into his mother are damaging to her: he may fear that these projections will be returned as attacks. In good circumstances, the mother will have received the baby's feelings, processed them for him with her own emotional capacities, and returned them to him in a form that he can manage. This process continues throughout life. It is hard to acknowledge the independent existence of those we depend on, because we are then afraid of abandonment. So we often deny the full independent humanity of others. Where we do recognize it—we feel the obligation to withdraw our projections, to seek containment in our own resources rather than expecting it in other people. This takes us from using the other to respecting him.

So it is my argument that to respect another person, several conditions are necessary. First we have to recognize the independent human status of the other, and then we have to strive to recall our projections from him and own them ourselves. An example of this would be a doctor projecting his own feelings of fear and impotence into his patient and treating them there rather than owning them himself. In order to treat the patient with respect, he has to recognize his human status, recall his own feelings of fear and impotence, hold and deal with them himself, and treat the patient in his own right.

It is very hard for us to maintain this attitude to other people. First, we become more aware of our own vulnerability to others, of our dependence on them and our emotional need for them. Second, we become affected by their lives; their pain and suffering has an impact on us. Third, we become aware of the effect we have on them, of how much we split off feelings we do not want and put them into others, and of how much they suffer from this kind of treatment. (In the example just mentioned, if the patient suffers from this treatment from the doctor, he is manoeuvred into feeling frightened and impotent.) Fourth, the task of recovering our feelings is an onerous one, difficult and painful to achieve. So it is hardly surprising that we are so reluctant to recognize the humanity of others and to do the internal work that is needed for us to respect them.

This analysis may strike some people as too complicated: respect, it may be said, consists simply in behaving properly to other people. I do not underestimate the importance of good practice and of guidelines to safeguard respectful behaviour, but if this behaviour is not underpinned by an internal conviction of the humanity of other people, it has no depth, and it can quickly be abandoned. Even when we have worked hard both to empathize with others and to withdraw our interference with them and so to develop this internal conviction, we can lose it very easily. So the situation, when the behaviour is not backed up by this conviction, is very precarious.

In traumatic situations on the NICU we find it hard to think of others as human, and where we do achieve this, we may lose it and thereby cease to respect them. The job is essentially about respect: to try in such a traumatic environment to treat babies as human beings, mothers as proper mothers, and families as the true environment of the baby; to help staff to treat each other with respect, and the families, who are in great pain, to treat the staff with respect. I refer to a "traumatic" environment but in many ways this goes counter to the atmosphere of the unit, which is one where the circumstance of babies in incubators who cannot be held by their mothers is treated as normal; staff come here to work every day, this is their ordinary life. And yet I believe that here in the middle of all this is a situation that is hard for us to look at and to bear, a situation where small vulnerable babies are exposed to considerable discomfort and at times terrible pain, unmitigated by the protection of the mother's body, uncomforted by her voice, not held by her eyes and mind. Of course, the mothers do visit their babies, talk to them, and think about them, but not in the continual way that would normally be the case.

I think this situation connects with our most primitive fears of abandonment and disintegration and that we meet it with fierce defences. Unfortunately these defences block our vision of ourselves and of the full humanity of the other people in this setting, so that situations arise where respect is not properly given. It is my job on the unit to provide some articulation of these fears of abandonment, to attempt some containment of unbearable fear and pain, and to help facilitate an atmosphere where there can be some mutual respect. I will try to make this vivid with the help of some examples.

* * *

First I want to write about the babies themselves. As is clear from the story above, the unit staff want to treat the babies with respect but have very different ideas about how to do so. Different ethical viewpoints clash fiercely, and people feel that their dearly held beliefs are not being given weight. Some would say that you respect a baby by not letting it suffer beyond a certain point, although where this point is may not be clear. Others feel that you can, without disrespect, withdraw treatment, while yet others feel that this withdrawal is itself an abandonment, and that you should ease a baby that is already dying towards its death. Others find this totally unacceptable, think of it as perhaps even murder, the use of a power to which we have no right. The NICU struggles with these questions. The issues are discussed each week at the psychosocial meeting attended by the doctors, the nurses, the social worker, health visitor, speech and language therapist, chaplain, psychiatrist, and the child psychotherapist.

A typical struggle about how to express respect can be seen in the following story:

> At the psychosocial meeting the consultant paediatrician announces that on the antenatal ward there is a 22-year-old mother whose baby is now at 25 weeks' gestation and has been found by ultrasound to be grossly abnormal. A decision has been made to terminate the pregnancy. Normally an injection of potassium would be made to kill the baby *in utero*, but emotionally this mother cannot bear that, so the birth of the baby will be induced and it will probably die in labour. However, there is a chance that it will live. The decision is that, should it live, it will be kept warm and comfortable but not artificially fed or ventilated. The news is initially met with silence. The consultant is asked for more information. The chaplain is asked to go and see the mother. A lot of sympathy and worries for the mother are expressed: she may need and get support now, but who, in the weeks, months, and years ahead, will be around when she needs help? The plight of this mother is felt to be so awful that it is hard to stay with it. We wonder if the situation has been caused by medical intervention. If she had not had the scan, she would have naturally aborted, or the baby would have been born grossly deformed. One of the staff asks whether it would have lived. The consultant says probably not, but that sometimes such children live for a few years, and in that time other ethical questions would arise: if a grossly damaged baby was admitted to hospital with an infection, then the question would be whether to withhold an antibiotic without which it might die or it might live and its condition be worse. So once again there is a question of whether or not to intervene. We remind ourselves that we would like some certainty about what it is "right" to do in these situations but that we are always faced by examples and counter-examples. The discussion becomes a more general one about the law in our search for some authority to take away the pain of bearing all of this.

Later in the day the nurses express anxiety that if the baby survives birth and the mother does not want it with her, it will be brought to the NICU. They protest that here they fight for life and cannot accept such a passive role towards a dying baby as just keeping it warm; will it be given pain relief, they ask. Then they insist that it cannot be in the nursery with the other mothers and babies, as this would be intolerable for the mothers, so it must go into a side nursery. As they calm down, they become upset for the young mother; they would like to discharge their anger on the consultant paediatrician, but they know that he is struggling.

Even as I record this, I feel proud of how hard the unit staff worked in this case to respect each other, the mother, and the baby, and proud of the degree of feeling and intelligence they used in thinking about these issues. At the end of the day they will have thought about this mother and baby, and they will also have looked after them. If the baby dies, they will lay him out with great care, take him to the morgue, and perhaps attend the funeral. The rituals that follow death are a relief—they are ways in which respect for the babies and their families and for the relationship that the staff had to them can be clearly expressed.

In this situation people were having to recognize that there were points of view different from their own. They were faced by a situation without hope: there would either be a dead or a very damaged baby. They often felt persecuted and wanted to find someone to blame. It would be easy for the feelings to become quite uncontained, and then persecution and blame would flourish. The discussions at meetings were an attempt to contain the unbearable feelings and gradually to own what was our own. Where this containment failed there would be a lack of respect. The complexity of these mechanisms within the unit is recognized, and the weekly psychosocial meeting is one place where these things can be thought about. At this meeting we discuss every baby in the unit, his physical progress, and his psychological and social situation. An attempt is made to think of the baby with respect as a small human person with certain needs. An attempt is also made to think about the parents and about how they are coping with this traumatic experience. The kinds of experience that we are trying to contain are ones that will almost certainly arouse very strong feelings in the group members. Here are some illustrations:

1. This unit serves the local women's prison; pregnant women in prison are more likely to have premature deliveries. When a woman from the prison with a baby is in the unit, there will be two warders with her.

    The unit has to work hard to contain its feelings about this situation. Some people may be overwhelmed with curiosity about the case. Some may empathize with the baby and be hostile to the mother. Some may feel heartbroken that this baby may only stay with its mother for a limited time, as this prison has a policy of keeping babies with their mothers in the prison mother-and-baby unit until they are 9 months old at most, and sometimes not at all. Some find the presence of the warders difficult or feel that the other mothers find the warders' presence difficult. And so on. It is the task of the unit meetings to allow these feelings expression, so that we can own them as ours and respect the mother and baby as human beings uncontaminated by our projections.

2. A mother is on the unit with twins with whom she does not seem to be bonding well. It is known that this is a gift pregnancy, that in fact the mother's best friend donated the eggs.

    In order for the staff to help this mother, they have to be able to imagine the difficulties involved in going through this kind of fertility treatment. They have to be aware of the sense of failure experienced by the parents in not conceiving in the ordinary way. The mother may have a task of mourning to achieve before she can accept these babies as hers. She has to give up the wish to have her own biological babies. She may wonder how she will face her best friend throughout life—perhaps wondering whether the children look like her. But these issues touch the rest of us at our own vulnerable places. The members of the group may want to retire into a self-congratulatory enumeration of their own children, or they may want to take refuge in humour or denial (e.g. what is all the fuss about? The task of the meeting is to discuss these issues respectfully without acting out private issues of our own.

3. A mother is on the unit with a very sick premature baby and feels this is a punishment for an earlier abortion.

    Within the group there will probably be people with all kinds of feelings about abortion. Some may themselves have had abortions, others may have had trouble conceiving and feel angry with people who have had abortions. There may be all kinds of religious and cultural attitudes, acknowledged and unacknowledged. But the task is to help this mother.

4. An allegedly psychotic mother is on the unit with a small premature baby. She has three older children, who are all in state care because she has failed to look after them. Social Services argue that she must be given a chance to take care of this baby and would take action only if she fails. The doctors feel that failure may entail the death of the baby.

    A case like this lends itself to conflict between the professionals. On the whole, Social Services, represented by a social worker from outside the unit, identify with the mother and want the mother to keep her baby, whereas the unit identifies with the baby and wants to protect it from danger. But the story hooks into the most primitive fantasies we have of being abandoned to a mad mother on the one hand and, on the other, having one's baby taken away because one is not thought to be sane enough to be a mother.

I could go on reciting cases like these—morally charged stories of conception, birth, paternity, fertility, madness, and abandonment. They are bound to affect every person on the unit. It is a hard task to own our own fantasies and to leave patients uncontaminated by them. It is particularly heroic to maintain respect when various defences offer themselves so readily. The medical setting encourages the staff to see themselves as the healthy grown-up people and the patients as sick, passive, and infantile, so the pressure to polarize in this way is great. Also, there is almost always a lot of work to do, so there is encouragement to take refuge from thinking in activity.

The psychosocial meeting is one place where this work goes on, but the nurses and doctors have also asked for support meetings in which to grapple with these issues. Both groups see the need for this, request it, and then find reasons not to attend: they are too busy, they forgot, they thought it had stopped, they had another meeting. But every now and then there is a meeting where people talk honestly about their feelings. One typical discussion centred around "Baby Sam", who was born with many problems including a very horrific skin deformation. The nurses wanted to talk about this but found it very hard. They said that at first they found him difficult to nurse, that they chose to wear gloves as they were afraid he might be infectious. But when they saw how much his parents loved him, they found that they could bear him better. Then they became quite angry with the rest of the world and said they objected to people staring at him, that they wanted to protect him from people's eyes. One nurse had pulled down the blind on the window, so that people could not look through. She insisted that he was human and that this unit was not a zoo. The atmosphere of the meeting was very heavy—there was no flow of conversation. It seemed that the nurses were grappling with thoughts of the monstrous and even wondering if this baby were human. When the mother found him loveable, they too seemed to be able to accept him, and then their first feelings were projected on to the onlookers. Fear had to be mastered before the baby could be respected, but then, to some extent, the outsiders were treated with disrespect—they became the receptacles for the nurses' curiosity, antipathy, and rejection.

There is also an issue about the parents respecting the doctors and nurses when the parents are in such a state of crisis. Some parents make a split between "good" nurses and "bad" nurses, and the bad become the dustbins for all their anger, exasperation, and hatred, leaving the "good" nurses clear to get on safely with the care of the baby. Usually the negative feelings have to be safely deposited in one place. The professionals have to struggle with deciphering whether these are fair criticisms or whether they are merely being dumped with the parents' anger. One father was famous for the rages he would fly into, and the nurses would dread caring for his baby. A nurse described how she felt after he had shouted at her and humiliated her in front of the whole nursery. She tried to understand this outburst but found the experience too shattering. This work to maintain or restore respect is carried out in the unit meetings.

I now want to consider more closely the impact on us of these very small, sick babies. There has been, in the literature, a lively controversy about the degree to which children feel pain, and until quite recently children would only infrequently be given pain relief for general surgery or opiate analgesia for invasive procedures on intensive care units. If this is the view for children, how much more it is the case for babies, and theoretical reasons have been advanced as to why infants may not feel pain. I discuss this in greater detail in chapter 5. It seems that paediatricians are often frightened of the clinical effects of opiates, despite research that shows that opiate analgesia actually reduces complications. But discussion of this topic may be obscured by our wish to deny that babies feel pain. It is hard for us to see and take in what is happening to them. Babies are alone in incubators, often in discomfort and subjected to painful invasive procedures. I have been told by junior doctors performing these procedures that to carry on, they have to block out the fact that these babies are babies. If a long line is troublesome to insert, if no good vein can be found, the doctor may begin to feel persecuted by the baby and to feel angry with it. To do this work, doctors probably need some degree of omnipotence or some temporary cessation of imagination, but then they are in danger of losing their respect for the baby. This may be only a temporary loss, and the more the doctor can own these feelings and discuss them securely, the more likely it is that they can recover their respect. But it is hard for young doctors, isolated at the bottom of a very hierarchical and competitive profession, to be able to acknowledge and describe these feelings. I want to describe an incident where the struggle for respect was harrowing.

* * *

This is an excerpt from my notes. "Jane" was a young woman senior house officer (SHO), and "John" was a very small premature baby.

> John was lying on his front. Head to the left—ventilator tied tightly into his mouth with the strings of his woolly hat. He was wearing only a nappy. Jane was on his right side and held his arm bent back behind him—she was examining his arm with a torch to find a vein. She said that she had tried to get the long line in twice and had failed. I could see John's face as I stood on the left side. She turned his arm, looking and looking. His face was twisted in agony; his mouth opened in a cry, but there was

no sound. His eyes were closed. His legs, shoulders, and other arm writhed as if trying to get rid of something. She let go for a minute, and he stopped screaming. She took up his arm again, and he began to writhe. She said, "You see, Maggie, you have to get the needle in gently, just through the wall of the vein so that you can insert the line—oh, there, I've burst it." Blood welled out, and she wiped it. I felt her pulling me to watch what she was doing, but I wanted to watch the baby's face. She said that the problem was that there really were not any good veins left—the senior doctor wanted the two good ones in his legs left in case another line had to go in. She looked over his legs and other arm and then back to the original arm. She held the torch against it, and John was writhing again. His face was creased up in pain. She inserted the needle, and his mouth opened again in this terrible noiseless scream. She said, "Oh, St Valentine's day—I was listening to the radio, I put it on to Kiss FM—anyway I'm working all day—today and Friday—I don't feel much like Valentine's Day—my car has broken down—everything." John's alarms went off, and she looked worried—what was going wrong with him? She wondered rather pointedly if the senior doctor was in the office. I offered to go and look, and she said with great relief, "Oh would you?" But he was not there.

I came back to her, and she said she'd try just one more time—that if you tried for too long, you just got into a bad state. As I looked at them, I did not know which one I felt more sorry for—they both seemed so desperate. Again John was writhing as she held his arm and screamed when the needle went in. Another SHO came in and said, "Oh Jane, can't you get it in?" She said that she could not, went on trying, and then gave up. She looked at the baby and said "You horrible little thing." I said that I had thought she must be feeling angry by now—she said that it was awful, that it made you hate the baby. Anthony, the other SHO, came over, and she said that she could put the baby through the mincer. He said that he would hold the light for her, and she tried again—this time John was screaming continuously. The two of them pored over him—Jane was whistling softly to the music. I began to feel quite sick. I wondered why people care so much about torture and yet allow this to go on. Jane failed again—and got up. Anthony took her place. He said something quite kindly about the little fellow and then added that he was misbehaving. Anthony set to; at one point he moved in rhythm with the music. He relentlessly continued while John writhed and screamed. Eventually he got it in. He looked up triumphantly and jigged around in his seat to the music. He said to a nurse that he should always play this music when he was trying to get in a long line.

Later that day we had the weekly junior doctors' support group, and the doctors talked about their need to block out their imagination and to concentrate on the task. They talked honestly about how persecuted they became by babies who were hard to treat, and how in spite of their rational self knowing that it was not the babies' fault, nonetheless they sometimes hated them, and how frightened they became of their own hatred. Some said they became persecuted by the nurses and began to imagine that the nurses were pulling out the long lines that they had so painstakingly got in. Also, they felt called from one place to another, interrupted, bleeped, and given no peace. They had to swallow their anger and worried about whether they took it all home with them. One woman doctor said that she had become possessed by the place. She would lie down to sleep, and these images would come to her. She could not say what they were, only that it was like a great octopus wound round you.

It seems to me that these doctors feel that they have to cut off from the babies' emotionality to do the job but are also aware of the pain they are inflicting on the vulnerable creatures who have no comfort, no refuge, and no containment. This makes them feel unbearably cruel and then they identify with the babies and feel cruelly persecuted themselves. There is an atmosphere of an absent mother. There is no mother to protect, to comfort, to digest the experience, and to ensure that the baby is not subjected to what it cannot manage. The junior doctors describe problems in their love lives, and I wonder whether this work undermines their belief in their own capacity to love and be loved. They identify so strongly with the babies that they often find it hard to leave the unit to go off duty; they describe themselves as bewildered by their own behaviour—that they hang around, have a cigarette—after doing long hours on call. Perhaps they have projected so much of themselves into the babies that it is hard to leave them.

Just as it can be denied that the babies feel physical pain, so it can be denied that they suffer emotional distress. The nurses know that they must encourage the mothers to "bond" and to visit frequently and to take as much care of the babies as they can. But the full extent of the babies' emotional deprivation is, I believe, denied. I think it is important to offer the babies some containment for their grief, their pain, their fear, otherwise they may have to erect very strong defences or dismantle their own burgeoning perceptions.

* * *

Here is an illustration of what I mean. "Ada" was born at 26 weeks with Escobar's syndrome. This meant that she had rocker feet and would probably never be able to walk, misshapen hands, and a deformed diaphragm. Her mother was devoted to her, and it seemed clear to me that the mother and baby girl were in love with one another. The mother found the splints that Ada had to wear on her arms and legs for a few hours each day very upsetting; she knew that they hurt Ada. There were questions about Ada's future: it was unclear whether an operation at Great Ormond Street Hospital to help her diaphragm was possible. In the meantime, Ada's personality gradually imposed itself on the unit. I found myself choosing to write up my notes beside her cot; I liked her company, and the nurses loved her. The mother, a proud, brave woman, quietly showed her devotion. Ada seemed to be doing quite well, but then she began to deteriorate. The mother was the first to notice this, but it soon became clear to others, and she was moved back into the more intensive care nursery. The doctors wondered what was wrong with her lungs, her heart seemed under great strain, and she was sweating a lot. Ada was taken for a second visit to Great Ormond Street Hospital for a reassessment. I knew that the mother hated this change of hospitals, and I decided to visit Ada there. As I went, I found myself wondering about making this visit to see a 5-month-old baby—whether this was a "good use of my time". Ada had had a tracheostomy two days before and was now being ventilated through a hole in her throat. These are excerpts from my diary:

> Mother sitting by the incubator—so sad—holding Ada's hand, stroking her. Ada holding on to her mother's fingers—every now and then opening her eyes to check on her mother. So painful to see this pain. Mother feels Ada has put up with enough pain—gone through too much. Mother was finding it hard to visit now, particularly if there was bad news. She seemed pleased that I had visited, and we agreed to meet the next day.

Next day:

> Mother was not there. . . . Ada had been back to the theatre because of problems with her trachy. She was asleep.

A few days later:

> Ada looked deep into my eyes with great concentration—very serious. She held her hands together, and when I put my finger towards her, she took it and held on. I talked to her, and she listened, sometimes furrowing her brow. She began to make a noise with her breathing, and her nose ran. I wiped it and talked to her.

> Every time someone came in, I looked up, hoping that it was Ada's mother. Ada's nurse came back and talked enthusiastically about Ada. But suddenly Ada began to cry. I wondered if I had disturbed her. Huge tears welled up in her eyes. The nurse checked different tubes, turned her on her other side. But Ada was still disturbed. The nurse said that she needed her mum, and where was her mum. My feelings very much echoed this. I became more and more uncomfortable as Ada was not comforted. Sweat was standing up on her forehead. The nurse wiped it gently away, and Ada calmed down a little. I left.

These extracts may give the impression that Ada's mother was not visiting often. In fact, she was a devoted attendant.

Ada returned to our unit, and after this my relationship with her became very serious. She was a lively baby loved by the nurses because of her responsiveness, her lovely smile and mischievous eyes. But she would fix me with large, serious eyes, and I would be drawn to talk to her, to stand by her cot to talk and to listen.

One day I went over to Ada's cot. As soon as our eyes met, she burst into tears. She did not stop until her mother arrived. I told her mother what had happened, struggling with guilty worries that I had made her cry. Mother said that she thought she often did not realize she was sad until someone spoke to her. On reflection, and with this help from her mother, I thought that I had enabled her to cry rather than that I had made her cry. In the days that followed, I would spend time with Ada talking to her and listening to her.

Ada demanded that her grief and pain be taken seriously. If her mother came late, she would turn away from her. If the doctors approached her to take blood, her eyes would fill with tears, and they would often postpone intervention because they hated hurting her. She would pull off the monitors and set off the alarms so that the nurses would come running, particularly at night when she seemed to want company. And she would roar with laughter. She would fix me with deep eyes, pull me towards her cot, and mumble away to me. I found it hard to leave her side.

Ada was often congested in her nose and throat, and the nurses would suction out the mucus. Although this gave her relief, Ada hated the discomfort of the procedure. One day she was congested, and I saw her mother bend down and put her mouth to Ada's nose and suck the mucus out. Later the nurse came to me in horror about this. But it seemed to me that the mother took on all of her daughter's experience. She did not just ask to be comforted by her daughter's smiles—she made herself the servant of all her experience and lived with her on the cutting edge of Ada's feelings, meeting Ada's need with her response.

Perhaps because of the extraordinary quality of her mother's love, Ada managed not to become an institutionalized baby. She played the clown and loved company, but she was discriminating and did not seek to please everyone. Her mother seemed to live and breathe for Ada and could also accept her own ambivalent feelings for her—for instance, she called her by an African name (her mother was Nigerian), which, we learnt, meant "messy".

A great worry emerged on the unit when Ada's first birthday came into sight. How in a neonatal unit could we give Ada the environment she needed? She could not go home, as she was on a ventilator and would probably always be. There were endless discussions at the unit meetings and with the parents. If she went to a long-stay children's unit, she would be far from her mother, but it was hard to see what else could happen. In the meantime Ada was sitting up in a chair in her cot, the queen of the nursery. But however much she would grow emotionally, her body remained malfunctioning. Ada solved the problem: one afternoon, some weeks before her first birthday, she pulled out the ventilator and died very quickly.

The unit went into mourning, experiencing guilt and grief and a whole range of feelings; even years later she is still spoken of and thought about. Ada was an unusual baby. She demanded respect, whether because of her own personality or her relationship with her mother, and she was respected. Seeing one who passed through in such a way, I realize how little we react to other babies, who do not have the same vibrant impact.

* * *

I have tried to describe a community grappling with issues of respect. I have used a psychoanalytic model to unpack the concept, arguing that respect for another involves appreciating him as another, an independent human being, and trying to keep him free from our projections. This involves containing our own feelings rather than using others to do so. Our capacity to do this may well depend on our experience of having our feelings contained by another (typically our mother) and our capacity to introject or take in this capacity. As I hope I have shown, we have many defences available against mental pain—notably splitting, projection, and denial, all of which lead to a loss of respect. A community such as the NICU has to institutionalize respect in the form of guidelines about "good practice", but, beyond that, respect demands an internal struggle to acknowledge the human reality of others, and of ourselves.

CHAPTER FIVE

Integrity

> To keep good and bad faith distinct costs a lot: it requires a
> decent sincerity or truthfulness with oneself, it demands a
> continual intellectual and mental effort.

> Primo Levi, *The Drowned and the Saved*, 1992

My argument in what follows is that the capacity for the
exercise of integrity rests fundamentally on the integration of the personality. I consider how this integration is
achieved and against what kinds of odds. This integration is then
tested continually in life by physically and psychically painful situations that tempt us to fly apart. My belief is that integrity is
located at this point—in the attempt to withstand this temptation
and to remain intact in the face of pain. The attack on integrity can
come from outside or from within: so we may be tempted to go
against what we know and believe because of the fear of threats or
mockery or because holding to what we know is psychically painful, or the attack may come from a split-off psychotic part of the
personality against which we are normally well armed. Right at
the beginning of life we work to integrate our different experiences

in order to gain an idea of ourselves and the world we live in. Alongside this work of integration, we usually split off into others unwanted and what are felt to be dangerous aspects of ourselves— for instance, hatred of those who care for and love us. So a later task of integration is to recall these alienated parts. It is this process and how it is related to integrity that interests me.

I hope to show, in the baby observations that follow, that the baby seeks integration, and this search needs an answer, something to meet his attempts, something to come up against, something for his searching mouth, eyes to meet his eyes. And this something is what gives meaning and pulls the baby together, as if acting like a magnet. Normally this would be the mother's arms, nipple, eyes, voice, smell, a mind to think and give meaning, and an ability to articulate this. So the baby has an innate impulse to integration, and the mother responds to this. This is both a physical and an emotional process. The physical gives rise to the possibility of integration, and the process of integration is emotional. The baby needs to be held and then is held—thus experiencing both the holding and the notion of someone thinking about what it is needing. The baby also has to sift out what is his and what is not, and in good circumstances the mother helps with this. The baby needs to know what are constructive, life-avowing impulses and what are destructive ones. On the NICU we often see mothers making such distinctions. One baby pulled out his ventilator, and the mother said in confidence that she thought that he had had enough and was giving up, whereas another baby pulled out her ventilator and breathed, and the mother saw this as a great step towards life. Of course, the mothers' judgements may be projections of their own feelings, but not usually. As the mother sees her baby in a life-and-death situation, she may see the struggle in him and try to support his life-seeking self. (Mothers sometimes feel that their babies are rightly giving up because the task is too much.) This integrating function, which is first embodied in the external responses, can then be internalized by the baby to strengthen his own attempts to integrate. So there is the growth of an integrative capacity, which can also sort out feelings and thoughts and know them for what they are—that is, know what is good and constructive and what is bad and destructive. So, for example, one might own racist thoughts (that is, not deny them or project them into others) but know them for the destructive, anti-life, anti-growth elements that they are. To deny the existence of these thoughts or to act on them would mean a loss of integrity, an abandonment of the integrative function, either because of the pain or because of the difficulty involved.

Implicit in all of this, there is quite clearly a moral theory that, I think, perhaps as child psychotherapists we tend to take for granted, but it may be important to enunciate it. We make a distinction between the good and the bad, between the impulse towards life and growth and the impulse towards death and destruction, and these are seen as closely linked to truth-telling and lying. The truth is thought of as food for the mind and good in itself, whereas lies are believed to be destructive and closely allied to perverse states of mind.

Then there is clearly a moral view about taking responsibility for oneself—owning what is one's own and not splitting it off into other people. When the baby is in a disintegrated state, we talk of him as having the idea of a good breast and a bad breast. Good here means something like gratifying, which is not a moral concept. As the baby heals the split between the "good" and the "bad" breast, and has an idea of his mother as a whole person, the space opens for anxiety about her, concern for her, worry about attacks made on her, gratitude for her strength and patience. The stage is set for the internal moral debate that will continue for the rest of the person's life. Here there is the struggle for integration and the retreat to disintegrated states of mind where a moral viewpoint can be ignored. Here the sifting out between truth on the one hand and lying and propaganda on the other takes place.

We have a life-long task of strengthening this integrative function and then of acting in harmony with it in ourselves. We are continually tempted to "go blind" on the things that we see, disintegrating where we had integrated, and I am arguing that integrity is found in resisting this temptation. Integrity here involves holding to our view, owning the often inevitable wish to go against it but not acting on that wish. In this view there is never a passive state of integration, because whatever we have achieved can always be challenged. And the task of integration is never fully achieved; it seems that there are always further unintegrated parts of ourselves. In my view integrity is located in the struggle to integrate, and this can never be wholly successful or fully achieved.

I consider this idea of integrity in the workings of the NICU, which is a particularly fraught workplace. Small premature and sick babies are treated, often with difficult and painful medical procedures. These test the babies' fragile attempts at integration. The mothers have to cope with high levels of uncertainty and with their own maternal needs being frustrated—they are not usually able to pick up their babies, hold them, feed them, and so on. The staff, both doctors and nurses, find themselves inevitably caring about these babies and their parents. They have to work quickly in situations that often have life-and-death consequences. The babies are extremely labile and can deteriorate astonishingly quickly— this makes the junior doctors in particular frightened and nervous. Furthermore, as I have mentioned in earlier chapters, ethical questions often arise where a practical decision has to be reached: When do you decide that a baby is in too much pain and should not be kept alive? Do you have to wait for a crisis, so that the baby can die because of lack of intervention? What do you do when a baby is very damaged, is not really viable, and is in pain, but the mother needs time to adjust herself to losing her baby and saying goodbye to it? These ethical questions are hard to face in the workplace where the consequences of one's actions are immediate. It is tempting to give oneself up to paranoid thinking and also to act so as to cover oneself in the law courts—that is, to protect oneself from blame at the cost of not following the best course of treatment. It takes integrity to stick with the real questions, particularly where there cannot be any "good" outcome. Such a fraught situation inevitably tests everyone's capacity to resist disintegration, and the hope of the staff acting with integrity rests on this resistance. Added to the difficulties of this situation is the impact of the Health Service reforms of both this and the previous government, which, I argue, encourage disintegration and thus undermine integrity.

There is also the question of research into pain relief for babies. As a spokesperson for the babies, I watch them and try to articulate their experience. Traditionally in medicine it has been thought that babies, and even children, do not feel pain. I think that it is hard for us to tolerate the thought of babies in pain, and so there has been a quite extraordinary denial in the face of evidence to the contrary and against the opinion of nurses and mothers. There are risks involved in using analgesia and anaesthetics in small babies, but these are offset medically by the intense stress response that can hinder recovery and may even cause long-term behavioural problems, and ethically by considerations about what kind of experience the baby is going through. Work done by Anand (1987, 1992) demonstrates these stress responses and how damaging they can be.

Rogers writes that it is

> commonplace for neonates to be rendered immobile or left awake or be given little pain relief during surgery in the belief that this practice minimizes the likelihood of anaesthesia-related complications. ... We persist in performing "minor" surgical procedures in infants ... without giving the same attention to relieving their pain that we give to relieving the pain of adults. ... It seems that we are better able to tolerate an infant's pain than to deal with our own discomfort and insecurity about the correct dose of pain medication to give the infant. [Rogers, 1992, p. 326]

Xenophon Giannakoulopoulis and colleagues (1994) have published findings about the response of foetuses to invasive procedures showing that the foetus raises a hormonal stress response to invasive procedures (for instance intra-uterine needling for foetal blood sampling) and that this response is similar to the hormonal responses mounted by older children and adults to stimuli that they would find painful. They call for further investigation into how these responses might be blunted by anaesthesia or analgesia. But in the same issue of *The Lancet*, D. A. Clarke writes in response:

> We all believe it worthwhile to avoid the experience of pain, although few of us would insist on morphine or general anaesthesia for simple dental procedure or for routine venepuncture. ... What do we know about consciousness of distress in utero, in contrast to the evidence that, as with any living being, there may be physiological responses to certain stimuli? Are there any short term or long term differences after birth be-

tween babies who have experienced stress due to intrahepatic vein sampling and babies who have not or who have had needling of their umbilical cord vessels? Is there a greater tendency to depressive illness, for example or evidence of impaired immune system function? [Clarke, 1994]

So these issues about the use of analgesia have been hotly debated. I think that it is distressing to accept that babies suffer pain, but there is a lack of integrity in going on acting as if babies do not feel pain when they cannot verbally inform us otherwise. So some doctors deny it, and the babies bear the consequences.

Therefore I see the first part of my job as keeping the babies in mind. In the second place, I have a responsibility to support the parents, to listen to their experience, and to help them make contact with their babies in the face of all this technology and institutionalized invasion. Often the mothers have not expected a premature labour and are in a state of shock. They have to bear their disappointment and put up with their anxiety about whether their new, tiny baby will live and whether he will be handicapped. And a large part of my work is to listen to mothers whose babies have died.

Third, I support the staff, both individually, if they ask for it, and in regular staff support meetings. I try to help them to keep fresh in their minds an awareness of the impact the babies have on them. The babies, not held or fed or protected by their mothers, often activate the most infantile terrors in those working with them: terrors of being abandoned by one's mother, being delivered over to an enemy or torturer with no protection, and so on. Honest junior doctors often admit to suffering from nightmares when they begin working on the unit. Even when they do not have nightmares, they may be bombarded by images of the babies at nighttime, and these often interfere with the few hours of sleep, which they desperately need for recuperation. My job is to help the doctors not to disintegrate by taking refuge in thinking of the babies as non-human little machines, or by overworking so that they no longer have time to think.

Of course, defences develop for reasons—sometimes good reasons. The doctors probably could not do their job without some defences. They need a temporary cessation of imagination. But if this becomes fixed, the doctor will become unable to act with integrity. He may become unable to sympathize with the baby, he may become highhanded and unable to understand the parents and their reactions, he may become bad-tempered with the nurses. Some doctors are able to talk to the babies, tell them what they are doing, and even apologize to them afterwards; thus a world of meaning is held on to and can perhaps begin to be established for the baby—a world in which there is some sense to all this and some hope, rather than a world of random pain or, worse still, a torture chamber. Of course, for the doctors and nurses to achieve this, they have to be able to bear enormous amounts of psychic pain themselves. They have to tolerate questioning their work, having others question it, caring about the babies and parents, going through the agony of thinking about this baby's life and grieving if it dies or lives in a handicapped state. They have to tolerate not being able to do what is expected of them and knowing that they may cause a death or worse by being slow or clumsy. Finally, if the baby goes home well, they have to hand the baby over to its real parents, often without having their emotional investment acknowledged. This is a setting that invites people to dismantle their minds, their feelings, and their imagination, but a price is paid by everyone if and when this becomes the culture of the unit. So my work at all levels of unit life is essentially about establishing integration and struggling to exercise integrity in the attempt to resist disintegration.

* * *

I will now move from this picture of the unit to a story of premature twins who were treated in our NICU. I first saw the "Suliman" twins as they were being wheeled into the NICU in incubators. There is usually an atmosphere of excitement and urgency around such arrivals. The staff then have to set to work, fixing the babies up with all the equipment they need in order to live. I subsequently heard about them at the weekly multidisciplinary meeting. These were boy twins of 24 weeks' gestation, who each weighed around 600 grams. Both parents were from Africa and had only lived in England for a short time. The mother, 24 years old, had previously had a miscarriage at 19 weeks of gestation. On the present occasion she had had to have labour induced because of infection, and the twins were given a rather grim prognosis. But Twin I was born in quite good condition, although somewhat battered. Twin II was stuck inside his mother, and an emergency Caesarean section was needed. However, at this point the mother was in a very bad state, hysterical and begging for an injection that would kill her. Eventually the father agreed to the section, and Twin II was born four and a half hours after his brother. It was noted that both parents had a sickle-cell trait. It later emerged that mother had had sickle-cell counselling in pregnancy and was offered the opportunity of a foetal blood test to allow a diagnosis of sickle-cell anaemia, in which case a termination would have been offered. Mother had refused these tests. Both twins were ventilated, and it was thought that their lungs were quite good.

I saw the mother on the postnatal ward. She sat slumped in a chair by her bed, saying very little. Eventually she said that she thought she could still feel the babies inside her. She was worried about why her husband was away so long at the telephone. I thought that the loss of her babies from inside her left her feeling confused and frightened. I arranged to meet mother and father together in a small room off the unit. I was struck by how much older than her 24 years mother looked. She spoke very little, and I wondered how much English she could understand. I imagined how frightening her labour must have been, so traumatic and in such foreign surroundings. The father greeted me in a very formal way, stretching wide his hands and making a speech. He asked me to thank the doctors who were, he knew, doing so much for their babies. This felt like a propitiation to some powerful authority in whose hands he felt himself and his family to be. I was to be the mediator. He went on to tell me about the labour and about the other baby that had died. He seemed to be in charge of his wife and her feelings. In the next few days he asked me what he should do about his wife's unhappiness. He wanted some method of getting rid of it, and he found it hard to wait and listen. I felt that he was rather bossy and dominating with his wife, but I reflected on how helpless he must feel. I asked the parents for permission to observe their twins, telling them that I was particularly interested in twins, and they readily agreed.

I started observing the twins when they were 2 weeks old. I have described the Tavistock model of baby observation in the Introduction to this book. It was in the tradition of this training that I undertook this observation. My one modification was that I took notes as I watched because I did not trust myself to remember accurately the little movements of these very premature babies. I went to observe Twin I, who had been named "Ahmed".

> He is under a layer of plastic. He has a ventilator to his mouth, goggles over his eyes because he is under a lamp to counteract jaundice. He is lying on his back on a nappy and is naked. His skin looks very dry and is very thin. He has heavy equipment on his left arm and leg. His face is turned towards the ventilator on his right. His right hand is bent over and goes up to touch his left ear, which is covered by some padding. His right hand moves around and touches his chin. Both feet flex. His right hand curls towards his mouth about three inches away from it. His mouth moves rather uncomfortably against the ventilator. He is still, and then his mouth opens on the ventilator. His feet are flexing. His right foot is moving against the sheet. He is still; after a while his mouth judders against the ventilator. His hand is now two inches from his mouth, and his fingers flex out a little very gently. His mouth moves on the ventilator, and his hand moves around. His mouth moves, closes, and opens rather slackly. He stretches his arms. And his right leg curls up into his open nappy. His right hand touches the ventilator and his mouth, then closes on to the ventilator near his mouth, and then rests against his open mouth. He explores his mouth and moves away. His hand goes back up against his mouth, his thumb goes into his mouth and his fingers against his cheek. Then his hand moves one inch away from his mouth with his index finger just touching the ventilator.

This observation continued, and I felt rapt and in awe of this little creature. His hand was like an adventurer in a new land, plotting the landscape, working hard to make essential links between parts of himself and between himself and the outside world. Here he was prematurely thrust on the shores of a new kind of world, in air now rather than water, having air pumped into his lungs. He no longer had his brother's intimate company or the steady beat of the placenta, although he did have the thumping of the ventilator. He seemed to be working out the relation of the ventilator to his mouth and to be establishing the link of his hand—or more particularly his thumb—to his mouth. Perhaps the link between his mouth and his hand was more familiar, and he was using this as the basis on which to go on to explore the link between his mouth and the ventilator. I thought that Ahmed was remarkably successful in striving for integration. His hand seemed to move with real intentionality.

I moved on to observe his brother, who was still unnamed.

His skin too is thin and dry. He is lying on his back on a nappy. He has on a hat which is tied under his chin and helps to hold the ventilator to his mouth. And he has a tube down his nose. His head is turned to the left. He has a lot of equipment attached to his left leg, which is straight down, and his right leg is bent up. His right hand is touching his penis. His right hand moves half an inch away, and his index finger is pointing to his penis. His penis moves and he is very still. Then his penis moves again very slightly. His left-hand fingers, which have to be straight because of the equipment, move against the bandaging. His penis moves back to touch his right hand—away and up—it is flexing as if it is searching for the hand—backwards and forwards. I find myself amazed. His hand moves slightly away. His penis moves up and down again and again and then touches his index finger and they stay together. His left leg jerks. He is still. Then his finger and penis move against each other. His hand bends over, and he touches his penis with his bent fingers. His left leg flexes up. He stretches all over—wriggling. Then his hand moves down and his bent fingers are against the length of his penis. His left leg straightens, and his right leg bends up. He is still and then after a pause he is wriggling. His nurse comes over and turns some equipment down, saying that it will be quieter for the poor child.

I am not sure what to say about such an observation. But I felt amazed by this little person. I felt convinced that I was not in the presence of random movements, but of a tremendous effort to

make connections, to make sense of himself, to explore, and perhaps to get some gratification or solace. He did not seem particularly uncomfortable or persecuted. I thought that he was full of
curiosity. The nurse was in tune with him, feeling his experience
and making him more comfortable. I think that the nurses are
more in touch with the babies when they, the babies, are in this
curious motivated state, and they are more likely to turn away
from them when they are irritable or have given themselves up to
mindlessness; or it might be that in this latter state they are in
touch and perhaps unable to cope with the babies' hopelessness. It
seems that the nurse and baby, as a couple, can get into a more
integrated relationship, more harmonious, when the nurse feels
able to help the baby.

I went to see Ahmed again a week later:

He is on his back, his face turned to the right. He has a hat on,
a dress lying over him, and a nappy on. The ventilator is
strapped to his mouth, and his left arm is under his dress. He is
now being fed from a tube going in through his mouth. He has
heavy equipment on his right hand. The nurse comes and
shields his eyes. I am hoping that they will open, but they do
not. He tries to bring his hand to his mouth, but he cannot
because of all the equipment. His feet curl up. His right hand
stretches out, his arm bending at the elbow. It tries again to
come to his mouth and then stretches away. He jerks. His right
foot beats against the sheet, and he rests. He judders. His
mouth, which has been open, opens further, and I can see his
tongue. His elbow bends, and his hand moves away from his
mouth. His tongue goes in and out. He is sucking his tongue
again and again. He stretches out his right foot, which is quite
badly scarred from blood-taking.

It seemed to me that Ahmed was frustrated in his usual activity of
getting his right hand or thumb into his mouth and that he beat his
foot in protest. Perhaps this gesture was to project the hurt or
frustration, and perhaps we can see here the building blocks from
which expression is built. The problem is that a projection of this
kind really needs an object that will receive it, and I thought of
how many times in the day Ahmed must have felt this kind of

frustration and tried to express it without anyone noticing. When I talked to the nurse about this, she said that he could not always have the equipment on the other hand. It seemed that Ahmed lost his way a little after this frustration and then concentrated on his tongue in his mouth. As the observation went on, he seemed to be exploring the inside of his mouth with his tongue and then to be filling the void of his mouth with it. The nurse told me that he was always pulling out his feeding tube. She readjusted it and told me that that morning, while she was doing something for him, he opened his eyes and looked at her. Ahmed was managing to put up with quite a lot of frustration and to continue his enquiries in the face of it. His concentration seemed to focus on exploring and filling his mouth and then gradually on his eyes.

By this time Twin II had been named "Tariq". I went to see him:

> He is lying on his back, his head turned to the right to the ventilator, which is in his mouth. He has a blanket over his legs, and his right leg is bent up. He has a hat and a nappy on. His right hand is against his right cheek, the fingers up towards his eye. His left hand is up against the back of his head. He is sucking on the ventilator, and then his tongue is sucking on the plastic of the ventilator. His mouth is opening and closing. The bleep on the machinery goes off. The nurse says that he certainly likes my company because his oxygen requirements have improved. Then he is still. It seems that his eyes are about to open, but they do not. He is sucking. The fingers of his right hand are under his eye, his hand arches out. The left hand, holding the back of his head, moves slightly. The nurse says that he likes to hear chatting around him. His right hand arches out again, and his left hand moves behind his head. His right hand moves down and he stretches, kicking the blanket off. His right-hand fingers go back to pointing to his eye. His eyes open in slits and close. His left-hand fingers move behind his head. Both hands move in a gesture to enclose his head. His eyes open in little slits, stay open, and then close. His hands move to enclose his head again. His right hand moves, and he is sucking. Both hands move, he is sucking, and his eyes open in slits. His hand goes to the plastic of the ventilator. His eyes open wider. His hand is on the ventilator, and his eyes open, close,

and open. His hand moves away and then back and then away and then further away and then back to the ventilator and rests against it. His tongue goes out to the plastic. His eyes open, and his hand moves just away from the ventilator and then right away. His tongue licks around his mouth. His hand comes against the ventilator and feels the part furthest from his mouth and then rests against the part that goes into his mouth. His tongue licks the inside of the plastic. My time is up, but I am reluctant to leave him.

I felt that what I saw was beautifully coordinated. Tariq took the momentous step of opening his eyes to this new world. I was moved by seeing his eyes open—it was a kind of birth, an entry into the world. It seemed that he had to hold on to his head with both hands while he was doing it—a gesture that is familiar to many of us when we have to do something difficult later in life. I wondered if this holding of the head was a very concrete kind of integration where the integrating centre, the head, had to be held together. It seemed then that he was exploring and integrating important zones and activities—his eyes and seeing, his mouth and sucking, and then there was the question of what he sucked on. He went away and came back, perhaps checking and perhaps gaining mastery. To watch a baby working in this way is riveting. There was also some acknowledgement by the nurse that this was a human baby who was reassured by human company and who thrived on hearing friendly voices around him.

By the time they were 6 weeks old, Tariq was in better health than Ahmed, though neither of them was doing as well as at first. They had both been on ventilators for several weeks, and their lungs were in a bad state. The staff felt that the parents did not understand how sick their boys were and that they were rather blasé. They only visited in the evenings.

In the seventh week I went to see Ahmed. I knew that during the previous week he had been on a mask. This is a less invasive form of ventilation, but the mask is strapped over the baby's face. Parents usually find this distressing and feel cut off from the baby, and I imagine the baby might have similar feelings. I also knew that he had a hernia and that his genitalia were very swollen. I found Ahmed covered by a light blanket to his neck:

His face is to the right and he has the ventilator to his mouth. He has the upper part of his open mouth against the plastic of the ventilator. I can see his tongue lying there inside his open mouth. He is very still. His eyelids move. A nurse puts an antibiotic in through a drip, uncovering his foot to do it. His eyes scrunch up a little as it goes in. His tongue goes into a V shape and then flattens out. He is very still. His tongue moves, and then his jaw makes rather strong sucking movements, almost like chewing. His eyes open for an instant while he sucks. His eyes open and close and then stay open. But they do not look focused. He blinks as though baffled by it all. They flutter and close. I found myself wondering if he is or will be blind. He is very still, with his mouth hanging open and his eyes closed. His mouth judders, and his eyelids scrunch up a little.

I felt that Ahmed was giving up his quest for integration. I felt overwhelmed by hopelessness and sorrow. Both he and Tariq, in observations at this time, seemed to have lost an exquisite intelligence they had had in the first weeks after birth, a natural will to explore and integrate. The world they—particularly Ahmed— were inhabiting now seemed to have lost its meaning, and he was disintegrating in the face of all his unbearable experience.

Ahmed became very sick. He had an infection; it was thought that this might be a fungal infection of the kidneys. His lungs were in a bad way. Meanwhile Tariq improved. The staff worried that mother did not realize what was going on. She visited very little. An attempt was made to get Ahmed on to a nasal prong, a more comfortable form of ventilation, but he could not manage and had to go back on to the ventilator. He was on a lot of antibiotics for all kinds of infections.

I went to see him in the 8th week, and he had both arms by his sides.

He is very still, with his eyes closed. As she attends him, the nurse yanks him with some equipment by mistake. He hardly seems to notice, yawns, and his right hand curls slightly. The nurse touches him, and he yawns again, his eyes opening a slit. The doctor gives him a heel prick for blood. He opens his eyes, his arms fly out, he screams and is quickly still again.

Probably the medication was making Ahmed sleepy, but there was a profound sense in which he seemed to have given up—as if the battle was too much. Pain was no longer something to protest against. It was thought that week that he would die. There was a lot of worry about whether the parents understood how grave his condition was. I had not seen mother for some time. I rang her and encouraged her to come in for a talk. It soon emerged that mother was not well herself and had been in hospital having a D&C, and that father was very nervous.

At 2½ months mother was visiting more and seemed more aware of what was happening. I met both parents. Mother talked about how special twins were in her culture: they were the dancers, and special songs were sung to them. She had not felt able to sing to them; I encouraged her to do so. She also talked about the baby she had miscarried and her belief that it had come back as one of the twins. By now Tariq was in a headbox, a Perspex box covering his head and shoulders, and mother could quite easily pick him up. One evening she picked him up and sang to him and was delighted that he looked up so intently at her. She was rapturous. With much more difficulty she picked up Ahmed, who was still ventilated. She sang a little to him but was afraid when he regurgitated some food.

The following week the registrar was very upset about Ahmed, telling me that he had a cyst on his brain and that she was not sure that treatment should be continued. I went to observe him. He was quite still, occasionally making little movements. I was taking my notes but found myself falling asleep. The nurse held his hand, saying that he knew when she talked to him and that he was worn out. Referring to the cyst, she said what a shame it was but that it might get better.

As Ahmed got sicker I found myself giving in to the temptation to disintegrate, to escape, when I observed him. I could feel myself giving up on watching, dreaming off somewhere else or falling asleep, or finding urgent reasons why I could not watch him, or falling into inane platitudes.

By Christmas the unit was in a state of torment about Ahmed. The consultant felt that it was cruel to go on treating him, that this amounted to torture. Some staff agreed, and some did not. He talked to the parents about the almost certain severe brain damage, and mother was devastated. I saw the parents, and father was once again very formal, wanting to thank the unit. He said that he was praying to God and that God could do anything. Mother agreed but said that Ahmed was in pain, that she pitied him, that he was going through too much. She said how joyful she had been to have twins; it made up for the lost baby. But this was too much. Father said that she had been suicidal and that he was afraid that she would walk into the road. She was worried about him, saying that he was a good man and should have children.

Tariq started to take some feeding bottles, otherwise he was fed through a nasogastric tube. I had seen him and the nurse enjoying a bottle-feed. This observation was made when he was nearly 3½ months old:

> He is lying on his tummy, and needs just a trickle of oxygen. His head is to the left, and his right hand is behind his head. His eyes are closed. He is breathing quite heavily. He screws his face up and sucks on the tubes. He begins squirming and wriggling and making uncomfortable noises. His left hand goes down, and his eyebrows go up. I am worried about the tube, which has fallen across his left eye, and I move it. He raises his head and buries it into the sheet, putting up his left hand. I think that he is looking for something to go into his mouth. He brings his hand to his mouth and nose and cries. He turns his head the other way. He seems to be searching—his right hand to his mouth and his left hand behind his head. This is a position that earlier in his life had given him comfort and held him together, but now he has had the experience of the teat in his mouth and sucking on it for milk, and that seems to be what he is looking for. He holds his right hand to his mouth and seems more concentrated, less bloated. He is still, and then his eyebrows go up and his eyes open slightly. His hand goes away, and again he is searching with his head into the sheet. His hand stretches up, feeling the sheet, touching his nose and then his ear. His head turns the other way. His left hand goes to his mouth.

> The nurse asks me if it is all right if she feeds him. I say of course, worrying whether she has felt inhibited by my pres-

ence. His left hand goes away from his mouth, and the nurse begins to put the feed down the tube. He wriggles. I ask the nurse about bottle-feeding. She says that he has about two bottles a day and is disparaging about how much he will take from a bottle. I feel critical because I have seen him enjoying a bottle so much, and I also feel that she could have taken him out for a cuddle while she is feeding him. Tariq cries and the nurse looks away into space while holding the tube. I feel sad that Tariq has nothing for his mouth and ask the nurse if he likes the bottle. She says, rather shamefaced, that he does, but adds that it is hard with the oxygen tube. She then asks me if I have recently seen the mother of a baby who died over a year ago on the unit. I think that she is telling me to stick to my own job or maybe telling me how it feels to be criticized, or shifting some responsibility to me, or maybe she is preparing herself for Ahmed dying. Tariq settles down with both hands in loose fists on either side of his head. He is still, and his mouth is jammed up against the sheet. He seems uncomfortable. He makes a noise and turns his head. The nurse continues to look away. His hand goes momentarily to his mouth. He grabs the tube. The nurse takes his hand away, and he cries and turns his head the other way. His left hand is exploring, and he is making a noise. He chokes. The nurse pats his body and he cries. He turns his head back to me, making noises with his mouth against the sheet. I find myself wanting to get away.

I thought that Tariq was desperately searching for an object—outside in the real world—to hold him together. Because he had had the experience of feeding from the bottle, this was probably the teat for his mouth, but it might have been arms around to hold him or other human eyes to look into and to have look back, or a voice to talk to him and to begin to make sense of his experience. I had seen him enjoying all of these things with the nurse the previous week, and at this stage it seemed that these were the things that he needed for integration; without them he became desperate, flailed around, cried, choked, and so on—the signs of what we commonly describe as falling apart. I thought that the nurse had likewise not been able to hold herself together. There was something here that she could not integrate, at least at this moment, and she had blotted out skills and sympathies that I knew she possessed. She probably knew, at least unconsciously, that she was doing this, because she evoked in me a sense of guilt that I think really belonged to her. What precisely she found unbearable I do not know; but it might have been the long haul that this baby had undergone, or the new sense of hope as he was progressing, or the contrast with his very sick brother, or the mother's absence; there may have been things going on in her own life that interfered with her capacity to understand and feel for him. Whatever it was, she did not manage to stave off this disintegration, and he lost the opportunity of some human contact, which he desperately needed. She did not manage it, and I did not help her. I think I allowed myself to enter the world of apportioning blame, and I think that she may have been driven further away by feeling my criticism. I think that Ahmed was my favourite twin—more splitting and a failure of integration—and perhaps I found it hard to see Tariq progressing while his brother was dying. This raises the difficulty we commonly have of thinking of one twin only in terms of the other.

Ahmed remained very ill. I saw that his tummy was very distended and that his genitalia were bloated from his hernia. The nurse looking after him was very gentle and told me that he was very irritable and sensitive to any handling. When the doctor took blood, his face screwed up in pain, and when the nurse touched his distended belly very gently, he looked as if he was gagging. Even in the middle of all of this his hand went to his mouth as if searching for something.

The next day I went to see him again.

He has his head to the right. He opens his eyes slightly from time to time. His tongue comes out, his mouth opens on the ventilator, and his tongue is mouthing. His eyes open slightly. He licks the ventilator strap and the plastic. His eyes open fleetingly, then stay open but are rather vacant. I find it hard to watch him and wonder if this is because he is dying. He is screaming as the nurse puts something down his drip. She comments that it stings him. She comforts him—rather roughly, I think—and then puts some more down. He is screaming again. She asks me if I have seen his right arm—it has become broken or dislocated. She does not know how, she has only just come on duty. She said that it hurts him when it is moved—she demonstrates, and he gives his noiseless cry. I ask her what it is like to nurse him, and she says that he is lovely, he has his own personality, and that he opens his eyes to see you. She adds that of course they are not sure that he can see. I ask if his belly is still distended, and she says that it is, adding that he is swollen all over. Ahmed closes his mouth on the plastic.

I thought about how I was about to go on a week's holiday and wondered if he would be dead by the time I came back. I wondered whether his parents would keep their appointment with me that morning and thought about ringing them. Then I found myself wondering whether I would ever write a book, and I imagined what the different chapters might be about. I became conscious of all this and realized that my mind was finding it hard to stay with Ahmed, that it kept on wandering away to escape or maybe to the possibility of another baby, which I thought was the significance of the book. With these reflections I found some strength to come back to Ahmed. The nurse asked me to move to the other side, because she wanted to do Ahmed's physiotherapy. She seemed rather cross, and she asked me sceptically whether I thought that Ahmed's parents would come to see me.

Ahmed does not seem to object to the physio—this involves his being thumped on the chest to break up the phlegm and dislodge it. The nurse says that she thinks that he quite likes it. As she works, she says that you wonder what you are doing— ethically—is it for the best? I notice how exhausted she looks and comment that she is looking after two very sick babies and that she looks very tired. She grins and says that she is. She has had two days off over Christmas and has spent most of the time on the motorway so that she could see her parents. Now she is back at work, and they are short-staffed. She says that at the moment work seems more like a test of endurance than a part of her life.

It seemed at first that the nurse had dismantled her own sensitivity and judgements and was full of inane comments, and then that she had given herself over to a cruel and meaningless world. She was a nurse whom I knew well and liked. She was generally thoughtful and very sensitive to the babies. Yet I was amazed to see her move Ahmed's arm so experimentally and to talk about his lovely personality in such a mindless way. As she did the physiotherapy, something seemed to come together for her, and she suddenly started talking about the morality of what was going on. Perhaps at the moment of feeling she could help him she felt less persecuted and could face this hard question. I think that I suddenly saw her struggling and could comment to her about how taxed she was. As she felt more looked after, her mood softened both to herself and to Ahmed. In the face of this pain and uncertainty it is tempting to forget all kinds of things that you do know, to doubt what you see, and to give yourself up to cruelty or mindlessness. It takes hard work to resist this or to retrieve a situation that is slipping downhill. I believe that the exercise of integrity is located here. As members of the unit, we knew very well the horrible complexity of the situation; all kinds of defences against this kept offering themselves to us, and the moral task was to try to resist these so as to treat Ahmed as well as we could. When we defended ourselves, bad treatment and bad decisions sometimes resulted.

While I was away for a week, Ahmed died. His parents were called in, and he was kept alive until they arrived. Both parents held him and wept. Then they disappeared, after giving the hospital chaplain thirty pounds to arrange a funeral and burial. He was upset feeling that Ahmed had been abandoned to him. The parents did not attend the funeral. Gradually we learnt that this was culturally normal for them and that the mother was not supposed to mourn her dead child because it might then come back. However, when mother reappeared on the unit, she asked me if I had attended the funeral, and when I said that I had not been able to do so, she seemed quite annoyed. I wondered if I was meant to do some of the mourning for Ahmed, and perhaps that is part of the function of writing about him now. Mothers with one dead twin and one surviving twin are faced with a particularly hard task of integration. It is very difficult to mourn for one baby and to pour one's energy into willing the other one to survive. Often mothers manage one of these tasks, but the other has to be postponed. In the next few weeks mother attended the unit daily, feeding Tariq, enjoying him, and looking very good. Tariq thrived, and it was soon time for him to go home.

Eight months later, I was sitting on the unit reading through my notes on Ahmed and Tariq in preparation for writing this chapter, and I saw some people walking past my table. It was Mr and Mrs Suliman and Tariq, coming to visit the unit to celebrate his first birthday. They looked happy and relaxed as the nurses chatted and cooed over Tariq. Father was suddenly serious and said that they wanted to thank the staff for saving his life. The Sulimans looked joyful on that day, but unfortunately Tariq has sickle-cell anaemia; it is not known how serious his condition is going to be, but he has already had a hospital admission with an attack. This means that his days of excruciating pain are not over. It also means that the doctors cannot reassure themselves that there was a happy ending to this difficult story. They are still left having to answer their own questions about what they have done. It takes integrity for them to face these questions in following up a baby's development into childhood and adolescence, since they can never be sure what the outcome of their work will be.

* * *

I have tried to describe an impressive and exquisite fight for integration on the part of the twins. It may be argued that we are fragile creatures and we cannot hope for integration. But I hope to have shown that even these most fragile and immature examples of our species are working away to make connections, to explore themselves and their setting. The sight of this work is very moving. It may be that in the face of such bravery followed by death, some would rather not admit that the babies feel pain or that they are having to deal with such a difficult experience, which may prove to be too much for them. But this involves issues about our own integration: whether we can manage to see what we see and know what we know, or whether we use one of the many mechanisms we have available to get rid of, deny, and so protect ourselves from what is painful to us. I have tried to describe how the staff struggle with and sometimes succumb to the pull to disintegrate in the face of pain. We may undermine our own perceptions, look the other way, fall asleep, or, like Mrs Suliman at one time, just stay away. If we succumb to this temptation, we may act with negligence or cruelty, and we have in effect abandoned the baby. We may also become brutalized so that nothing moves us any more. These are states of mind that we all fall into at times, but there is a question of whether we can recover from them. We may find the situation so unbearable that we have to find someone to blame—for instance, the parents, the other staff, the obstetricians, the doctor who resuscitated the baby in the first place, the doctor who did not resuscitate the baby quickly enough, the ambulance men: the candidates go on indefinitely. It is hard to take responsibility for what is happening and not try to shunt the blame off somewhere else. This again involves integrity. The other side of this is to idealize the unit, to think of ourselves as a well-intentioned group of expert and devoted people struggling in severe conditions—a kind of Second World War mentality that can make one feel comfortable.

The NHS reforms brought in by the previous Conservative government, which have been changed and extended by this government, have certainly made matters worse. In the market economy ethos and with the trust system, units compete with one another, and there is a question of who can deliver the best service most cheaply. Colleagues who were friends and collaborators have become economic rivals. It has been known for one unit to spy on another to see how it is cutting down its costs. Staffing levels are cut to a minimum, which inevitably means that agency staff have to be called in. These are sometimes less well trained nurses but, perhaps more importantly, they are not part of the team. A team has to grow together, with people getting to know each other so that there can be trust and cooperation. With a large number of agency staff, communication suffers, and an even greater strain is put on the permanent staff. But beyond this, a view is fostered that one individual can be slotted into another individual's place without any bad effects; the consequent deterioration in human relationships is ignored. There is, in any case, a constant pressure in the Health Service to think in this way; the nurses do not stay with one baby for too many shifts, with the intention that they should not get overly attached; junior doctors are moved on to a new job very quickly. This has always been true in the NHS, but it has certainly been exacerbated by the reforms. This means that there is a continual wearing away of attachment, a trivialization of human contact. This situation makes the struggle for integrity even more difficult.

In this fraught and economically competitive situation it is seen as an act of great disloyalty to say anything critical about the unit; a picture of "everything being fine" has to be maintained. We cannot "afford" to have our public image tarnished. Any criticism amounts both to suicide and to a murderous attack on the unit. So people mutter about unsafe staffing levels, but these criticisms must not be openly voiced. Attempts must be made to hide from parents that the situation may even be unsafe for their child. And everyone goes in fear of anything being leaked to the press. Along with this go mutinous wishes that the parents would complain to the press and the whole thing be exposed. This competitive system does not facilitate an open discussion of our problems and an honest acknowledgement of negative feelings.

Over the last forty years complex structures have been developed in the Health Service. Child psychiatrists and child psychotherapists have encouraged an integrated view of the child. This means that the child, not the symptom, gets treated. The child in his family, in his school, in the community gets thought about. This needs a lot of time-consuming liaison work but leads to much better practice. The delicate balance of this kind of work has been wrecked by the new way of thinking. Money, which has always been tight, seems to be more scarce and has become the dominant consideration, and there are no longer the resources or the ideology required for thinking in this integrated multidisciplinary way. This is a plain pull away from integrity, so that we no longer think in terms of the health and wellbeing of our citizens but of the best delivery of a service—for instance, the ventilation of a baby. Of course, a unit such as the one in which I work in tries to continue with its tradition, but in the face of enormous opposition. The job security of link workers like speech therapists, health visitors, social workers, child psychiatrists, and child psychotherapists is precarious, and most of these people have had their workload increased, so that they cannot deliver anything like such a thoughtful service. This attack on thought seems to me to be the crucial point. In a situation under such economic pressure it is difficult to find time to think. Exhausted doctors and nurses find it hard to change gear to reflect on their cases and to attend staff support meetings. This is a culture-wide problem, and it may be that the injustice, destructiveness, and cruelty in the way human beings are being thought about in our society at present is very painful to admit to, and so we stop thinking and give up on our integrity.

I do not believe that the NHS is being destroyed just by lack of funds. There have always been and always will be situations where money is short and choices have to be made about what we can afford and what we cannot; and neonatal intensive care units may be something we cannot afford—in which case this needs to be said carefully and clearly. I am arguing, rather, that the atmosphere of economic competition in institutions designed to provide health care runs counter to the difficult task of thinking about people in an integrated way as human beings. To send a mother back to a local hospital from a more specialized hospital after a few weeks may make economic sense, but it may not make emotional sense—the mother has experienced a premature birth, and she is being held and helped to get to know her baby in very difficult circumstances; to send her somewhere else can undermine this restorative work. Ironically, it is probable that looking after people properly and considerately is cheaper in the long run, and the mechanical treatment that is becoming commonplace just piles up more and more of the social and legal problems with which we are becoming so familiar, and which are so costly. It might be argued that I am expecting a degree of integrated thinking from management or government, which it cannot achieve, that it is too big or too institutionalized. To that I would say that we are talking about degrees here, and that it may be that institutions by their nature run against integration, but we can still work to lessen this.

Postscript

Turning and turning in the widening gyre
The falcon cannot hear the falconer;
Things fall apart; the centre cannot hold;
Mere anarchy is loosed upon the world . . .

Yeats, *The Second Coming*

When I began to write this chapter, fragments of the first four lines of this poem by Yeats kept coming into my mind. They seemed to describe so well the states of disintegration that I was thinking about. The image of the falcon and the falconer made me think of the baby needing to hear the mother, to be held in against the desolation of the "widening gyre". I thought also of the centre of one's personality—the strength one has been given to take on more and more of oneself, to own it and not to have to send it off into others—and of the mess when this centre cannot hold.

So I looked up the poem to remind myself of the rest, and found it not so comfortable. I could not understand it. I wondered whom I could ask to explain it to me. I remembered not liking Yeats's poem to his newborn daughter, with its emphasis on privileged innocence—it seemed a rather attenuated life that he was wishing on her—and here again was this valuing of innocence. And then I began to think about integrity and the project to call in unknown parts of oneself and to get to know them. It sounds quite friendly. But I remembered several experiences in the analytic setting—some as therapist, some as patient—of being very frightened of something emerging: perhaps some rough beast. If we are really committed to integration, we cannot know what will emerge, we have to tolerate the unknown. We cannot ask for any insurance policies, we can only trust to the goodness and strength of our internal objects—by which I mean our internal resources built up from the positive assimilation of good experiences.

I worked recently with a pregnant woman who had been told that her baby was going to be very disfigured. She was given the opportunity of an abortion, but eventually she decided against it. Weeks passed, with more tests done and a very bleak forecast. When she was well past the time when she could have an abortion, she arrived at the hospital in a deranged state, demanding an abortion. The next few weeks were hell for her. I think she felt so mad because she thought she was carrying around a monster inside her. When a human little girl was born, admittedly with many deformities, the mother was overjoyed and put her to the breast.

I think that, likewise, we are afraid of integration because we are afraid that inside somewhere there is a part of us that is not human but monstrous, the fiend within. Added to this there are the dangers of a false integration: for instance, a sort of law-and-order mentality that holds us together falsely by fear and power rather than by understanding. If someone acted in a behaviourally correct way but was driven by a harsh superego, I do not think that it would be correct to describe him as acting with integrity—he would be acting from, say, fear rather than from a moral view that he had integrated and that, he felt, was worth striving for. To distinguish the true from the false, we have to develop our capacity to hear when we are lying to ourselves. This is no easy matter, and, as with this poem, we may find ourselves baffled. But not even to aspire to such a project of integrity leaves the rest of the world at the mercy of all that we have disowned and of our blind selves.

CHAPTER SIX

The struggle of life and death wishes

No more bee greev'd at that which thou hast done
Roses have thorns, and silver fountaines mud,
Clouds and eclipses staine both Moone and Sunne,
And loathsome canker lives in sweetest bud.

Shakespeare, Sonnet 35

In fourteenth- and fifteenth-century Italian painting, there is a tradition according to which the Virgin receives the Annunciation in five different and successive modes—Disquiet, Reflection, Inquiry, Submission, and Merit (Baxandall, 1972). It was thought that she had to work her way through all of these reactions. If we look at some of these paintings, we see that the artist conceived her state of mind in many different ways, far overstepping the limits of this tradition.

Fra Filippo Lippi's *Annunciation* (Figure 6) shows the Virgin's submission; the angel bends towards her gently knowing the heavy import of what he has to say. In Fra Angelico's fresco in San Marco (Figure 7), the Virgin's body seems to submit; her hands are perhaps protecting her, but her face is full of an acceptance with yearning to understand what is being said. Contrast both of these

Figure 6.   Fra Filippo Lippi, *The Annunciation*
(National Gallery, London).

with the earlier painting by Simone Martini (Figure 8), where the
Virgin recoils aghast and the angel seems full of foreboding. In
Piero della Francesca's painting (Figure 9), the Virgin does not
show such violent revulsion, but she looks disturbed and proud—
as if she knows that her life will never be the same again. The
Archangel Gabriel is solemn and restrained, and, above them, God
the Father ordains how things shall be. Earlier yet, Duccio (Figure
10) shows Mary submitting, perhaps cowering and troubled, and
the angel as determined and rather unsympathetic. With Tintoretto (Figure 11), we have a clear portrayal of the thunderbolt that
burst into Mary's life, knocking her off balance and interrupting
her life. The movement of the dove, perhaps symbolizing in this
picture the conception, has a direct and even aggressive quality.
My point is that tradition gave a rather acceptable list of Mary's
feelings, but these painters had a more lively idea of what all this
might have meant to her.

It seems important to remember that a woman greets the news
of pregnancy with a rich variety of feelings. Most little girls play at
being mothers, so pregnancy and mothering have been a woman's
preoccupation on and off for many years. In her fantasy she may
have modelled herself on her own mother, using her own experience of her mothering in her play. She may feel that she will do
much better than her mother had done, or plan to be the complete

opposite. Faced by the reality of her own pregnancy, she may be overjoyed, full of wonder, excitement, and plans; at other times she will probably be afraid and even filled with revulsion. These fears are often hard for a woman to admit to anyone—sometimes even to herself. They spring in part from her own childhood preoccupations: how will the baby get out, how did it get in—that is, what sort of conception was it—how will she be able to look after the baby, has she now got to give up her own girlhood, will nothing ever be the same again? This latter thought is an important aspect of pregnancy—mourning for the carefree life that is over or for the freedom to concentrate on her own preoccupations and interests. It is noticeable that in several of the paintings we looked at, Mary is interrupted in her reading. Women faced even by a wanted pregnancy often feel interrupted in their own intellectual and sensual pursuits and fear that they will never be able to return to these.

Figure 7.   Fra Angelico, *The Annunciation to Mary*
(Monastery of San Marco, Florence).

Figure 8.   Simone Martini, *Annunciation*
(Galleria degli Uffizi, Florence).

The pregnancy is an intrusion not only into the woman's body, but also into her mind. And in these paintings, the rays from God as a Dove or Holy Spirit are sometimes directed to her womb and sometimes to her head. If the mother is able to admit to some of these feelings within herself, she is probably more prepared to receive her baby as it is rather than in the idealized form in which she sometimes thinks of it.

At times the mother may feel that she does not like the baby inside her—who is this alien creature who is invading her? And with this may come all kinds of worries about whether it is well formed or a monster. An awareness of her own hostile feelings may make her feel very protective and worried for her baby. Where she can bear her own ambivalence, she can grow in her own reflectiveness, in what has been called a capacity for reverie. One of the most difficult and painful tasks for a mother is to recognize her own murderous feelings towards this creature, who often is also the most precious thing in the world to her. In our culture we are very bad at helping mothers with all of this. Advertising con-

Figure 9.   Piero della Francesca, *Annunciation*
(San Francesco, Arrezzo)

Figure 10.   Duccio di Buoninsegna, *The Annunciation*
(National Gallery, London).

tinually bombards us with idealized and sentimental pictures of
motherhood—images that give no idea of the enormous mental
work that is involved in mothering. So many women get no help
that could enable them to cope with feelings that they find in
themselves and are frightened by. They may secretly feel criminal,
they may try to split these feelings off into other women and hate
and fear them, they may try to deny them and overcompensate by

giving more and more to their children in the hope that this will make everything all right.

In the Bible we read that after the Annunciation Mary hurried to talk to her cousin Elisabeth, who had also heard that she was herself pregnant, although she had thought that she was past child-bearing. In Albertinelli's painting (Figure 12), we see a concerned Elisabeth welcoming Mary. They grasp hands in a comradely understanding of need, and Elisabeth puts a hand of comfort on Mary's arm. Mary looks deep into Elisabeth's face, I think for comfort and support, and her left hand rather tentatively fingers her own scarf. The wonderfully rich colours of this painting add to our sense of the depth of feeling between these two women and their growing awareness of what they are involved in. In

Figure 11.   Tintoretto (Jacopo Robusti), *The Annunciation to Mary* (Scuola Grande di San Rocco, Sala Inferiore, Venice).

Figure 12.   Mariotto Albertinelli, *The Visitation*
(Galleria degli Uffizi, Florence).

Giotto's painting (Figure 13), Elisabeth greets Mary with great concern, understanding something of what she is going through.

In pregnancy, women often turn to other women for reassurance and comfort. They have some hope that another woman might be able to help them with feelings that they are finding too puzzling. Mrs "Adams", a young woman who had always liked small children and had longed to have babies of her own, was horrified to find how hostile she felt when she discovered her pregnancy. Children she saw on the way to work who had been a source of pleasure became the objects of murderous thoughts. She told her news to an older woman friend, who both understood her hostility and was celebratory of the pregnancy, and with great relief Mrs Adams was able to find her own joy and excitement about the new baby.

Figure 13.   Giotto di Bondone, *The Visitation of Mary*
(Scrovegni Chapel, Padua).

Figure 14.   Piero della Francesca, *Madonna del Parto*
(Cappela del Cimitero, Monterchi, Arezzo).

But Mary did not stay with Elisabeth. She returned home, and
the Bible describes her as brooding on all these things in her heart.
In the *Madonna del Parto* by Piero della Francesca (Figure 14), we
see Mary, heavy with child, standing solidly, lightly feeling her
baby, and gazing full of thought. Her eyes are slightly out of focus,
one cast down and the other more outwards, which gives her the
appearance of looking both inwards and outwards. This picture is
now in Borgo San Sepulchro, but you used to have to search the
Tuscan countryside to see it; eventually you found a little chapel in
the hills, you entered the chapel and were faced by the painting.
The two angels hold open the curtains. It seems that Mary's dress
is splitting open and that she will split open to give birth. We see
Mary here in her inmost reverie, solidly facing thoughts and feel-

ings that are new and unexpected—it is a look that I have particularly seen on many pregnant women's faces.

The Madonna del Parto reminds me of another set of paintings, the *Madonna della Misericordia* (Figure 15). Here the Virgin shelters all of humanity under her cloak. Again, in Piero's version, we see her lost in thought. Where does she get her resources from, who supports her, how can she manage this burden? These thoughts are very common to mothers—how will they manage, will there be enough, who will help them, there seem so many people to look

Figure 15.   Piero della Francesca, *The Madonna of the Protecting Cloak, with Saints* (Polyptych, Compagnia della Misericordia, Borgo Sansepolcro).

after. It has been pointed out that the Virgin's head and the outermost points of her cloak form a triangle like the Trinity, and perhaps there is some idea of Mary supported by God the Father. In all this reverie women are relying both on their own internal strengths and on their external support.

Many women become worried during pregnancy and postnatally about their own resources and those of the world. Mrs "Barnes" with a new and premature baby in the NICU worried about how she would have enough time and strength for her 2-year-old. Mrs "Evans" (see chapter 7), whose first baby had suddenly died at five months, was afraid, when she became pregnant, that she would not have enough love for the two babies—either she would be disloyal to her first, dead, baby or she would not be able to love the new baby, who, she would feel, was an intrusion into her conversations with and thoughts about her first baby.

Perhaps the *Madonna della Misericordia* paintings represent some wish we have for an all-loving, all-encircling, all-giving Earth Mother. Many women think that they should fill this impossible role and are terrified. Perhaps those paintings that show the Virgin's breast spouting milk are magical fantasies that the resources will not fail. Mothers are often afraid that their milk will run out, or that it is poisoned because of the bad thoughts they have been having. Sometimes mothers are afraid to breast-feed. They cannot believe in the goodness of what comes from inside them. We hear of mothers being convinced that their milk is giving their baby terrible tummy-ache, or an allergy, or that it is too weak to satisfy their baby's hunger. Of course, these things may be true, but they are very rarely so. The mother may have all kinds of fantasies about her milk, about whether it is contaminated by bad thoughts, and about whether it is adequate. She will also have thoughts about her baby—that he will suck her dry so she has nothing left, that he will get too close, so that the relationship feels frighteningly sexual. The possibilities are endless, and they are all just the beginning of this mother and this baby getting to know one another. In a manic attempt to allay these worries, some mothers take on mothering the whole world, and in a rather masochistic way sacrifice their own needs to serving others. I think there is an aspect of this in the *Madonna della Misericordia*—Mary crucifying herself in the service of all humanity.

Figure 16.   Leonardo da Vinci, *The Virgin and Child, with Saint Anne and Saint John the Baptist* (National Gallery, London).

A very real and reassuring idea of support is present in Leonardo's cartoon (Figure 16). This is a most beautiful picture, with Mary sitting on her mother's lap. St Anne is looking at her daughter with great love, and Mary is looking at her own child. St Anne appears as a young woman, although not as young as Mary, and perhaps she appears as Mary would have remembered her looking when Mary was a little girl. I think this is the most wonderful depiction of the new mother relying on her experience of being loved and mothered in order to be able to love her own child. We see St Anne able to be in the background—I would see her as Mary's internalized mother—looking at her with such pride and joy in her motherhood, encouraging and allowing this new role. It seems particularly meaningful that Mary is sitting on her mother's lap. I think St Anne is giving her daughter a lap, and this is support, love, flexibility, and the ability to subordinate one's own ego to the needs of one's daughter. We also see a mysterious pointing left hand, which seems to belong to St Anne and yet is clearly not her left hand. Perhaps this is an idea of Mary's internal father, who with St Anne makes a combined parental couple that can support her.

Many of the mothers whom we see in hospital or at home do not have their own mothers or fathers around. Of course, they all have internal mothers, and these may be more or less supportive to them. But I think this idea of a lap is a useful one for us to think about. For the mothers on the NICU the unit may be a lap, or a particular nurse or doctor may be; a midwife, health visitor, or breast-feeding counsellor may give this support. I think what the Leonardo picture shows so beautifully is that it is support of the whole woman; and St Anne is a more shadowy figure—she can give herself in service and not spoil her daughter's realization of herself as a mother. This is a very particular and difficult grand-motherly task—because there is still, even in the grandmother, that little girl who wants to be the most perfect mother, better than her own mother and better than her daughter, that competitive even envious streak with which most women have to struggle. This pitfall for grandmothers is there for anyone seeking to support the new mother—the task of giving oneself in service and at the same time taking a back seat is a hard one.

Giulio Romano's drawing (Figure 17) also shows Mary sitting on her mother's lap. Joseph is holding a frame, which he has presumably made to help Jesus learn to walk. Fathers are clearly vital in the task of supporting mothers' mothering; they often take on a very nurturing role, and to do this well, they have to reconcile themselves with their competitiveness with the breast-feeding mother's unique relationship with her baby. So we sometimes see fathers who try to take over the breast-feeding, to be the manager and in charge of it, or who undermine the activity. Other support-ers can ease this somewhat by being very careful to recognize the father's importance in his own right and not to make him feel an intruder into his own baby's life. It is tempting for the female

Figure 17.   Giulio Romano, *The Holy Family and St. Anne with the Christ Child about to be taught to walk* (Chatsworth).

supporter, who may already be feeling jealous of the mother's special place with the baby, to split these feelings off into the father and to make the nursery a female environment, with the men outside, carrying the feelings of being left out. In this picture St Anne has drawn back away from her daughter and her new family—she even looks rather angry; perhaps it is easier for the grandmother to support her daughter in her mothering, to become her partner in this, and more difficult to allow her son-in-law in to find his place. It seems to me that the Romano sketch shows another important job that the father performs, which is to be the person who introduces the baby to the outside world. The baby is intimate with the mother, but the father opens up a space for new and different thoughts, a space for exploration of the outside world.

As I thought about writing this chapter, I remembered conversations I had had with mothers with new babies on the NICU, on the postnatal ward, and when doing ordinary baby observations in people's homes. What strikes me is the complexity of thought and fantasy that the mothers express. There is all the joy, the excitement, the wonder. But this is also a new love, and with it comes all the fear of loss—will the baby be all right, will it live, will the world be a peaceful place for it to grow in? If the child has a handicap, there will be all kinds of anxieties—will it get teased at school, who will look after it when the parents get old and die, how will it manage its life, will its life be a burden to it? These thoughts pass through the mothers' minds, and they have to bear them as best they can. I have noticed that mothers are often particularly keen to talk, while they are actually breast-feeding, about things that are worrying them. One mother, who had lost a child in a car crash in which she had also been very badly hurt, would pour out her grief once her new baby was sucking steadily at the breast.

A mother with a new baby is often in a state of heightened emotionality. This is the beginning of her motherly task of loving this child and bearing whatever comes up. In art I think we see this most movingly portrayed in pictures of the Virgin and child. When we first look at these Renaissance pictures, we are struck by their beauty, but on closer examination we are often aware of a look of great thoughtfulness on the Virgin's face. Then one sees within the painting symbols of the future. In *The Virgin and Child* by Masaccio (Figure 18), we see Christ eating the grapes symbolizing his passion. Mary holds the grapes for him and looks rather blankly away. Her body seems to hold him, and she, in turn, is held by a very solid chair. The angels play their instruments, and one is left hoping that this music is helpful to Mary. Jesus seems to get on with the business of taking in the grapes. In the *Virgin in the Meadow* (Figure 19) by Raphael we see St John offering Christ the cross, which he accepts. Mary watches over this, taking it in and seeking to support him with her arms and legs. Then there is the powerful *Mary, Child, and Saints* by Piero della Francesca (Figure 20), which has an egg, the symbol of life, suspended above the Virgin and Child, and a coral necklace, symbolizing the sacrifice, around Jesus's neck. Here the baby Jesus looks as if he were already dead. Piero, I think, shows unsentimentally what a desperate struggle it is for Mary to hold all of these things in her mind. In his painting she seems to be in danger of being overwhelmed by

Figure 18.   Masaccio di S. Giovanni, *The Virgin and Child*
(National Gallery, London).

despair—for the moment she cannot hold her baby, she can barely cope with herself.

This idea is also present in Bellini's painting, the *Madonna of the Meadow*, in the National Gallery (Figure 21). Again we see Jesus, the baby, lying on Mary's lap in a way that cannot but remind us of the pietà. Mary seems unable to hold her baby to her, and he is in

Figure 19.   Raphael, *Virgin in the Meadow*
(Kunsthistorisches Museum, Vienna).

danger of falling off her lap. She has retreated into prayer, and
there is little comfort to be had from those around her. It seems
that, in the full flush of love for her new baby, Mary knows in some
form what lies ahead and is having to cope with it. This seems a
very fundamental parental task. In the background of this painting, normal agricultural life continues. This reminds me of the
many mothers who are suffering and who have said to me that
they are amazed that the world has not stopped. One wonders

how Mary can cope with her knowledge of what lies ahead. In many of these paintings we see the beautiful and peaceful Tuscan countryside behind her and maybe this is sustaining, and in the Leonardo cartoon she has her mother, St Anne, as a support. She had her cousin Elisabeth to talk to, and St Joseph. She had external support and her look of contemplation suggests this internalized

Figure 20.   Piero della Francesca, *Mary and Child between Angels and Saint John the Baptist, Bernardin of Siena, Hieronymus, Francis of Assisi, Peter the Martyr & John the Evangelist, and the donor Federigo di Montefeltro* (from the church of San Bernardino, Urbino, Milan, Pinacoteca di Brera, Milan).

Figure 21.   Giovanni Bellini, *Madonna of the Meadow*
(National Gallery, London).

into inner strength. As the Piero picture shows, she is holding
together all the hope of new life with thoughts of death.

We know from clinical work how hard it is for a pregnant
mother to have to cope with a death. It may be that this can even
lead to a miscarriage or to premature birth. Mrs "Dillon's" beloved
father-in-law died when she was in her fourth month of pregnancy. Her baby stopped growing, and there was some discussion
of a termination, which was rejected. However, the baby was born
at 28 weeks of gestation, struggled for a few weeks, and died. As I
wrote in chapter 6, women who have twins one of whom lives and
the other dies have a particularly hard task: how to mourn and to
rejoice in new life simultaneously. This is particularly dreadful
when one twin dies *in utero* and for a while the mother is carrying
one live and one dead twin. But apart from these more extreme

cases, there is often a combination of lively and deathly thoughts in the new mother. The new baby seems to push the generations on, to make the mother's own mother a grandmother and so nearer to death.

A painting that I find puzzling is Piero della Francesca's *Nativity* (Figure 22). I have found myself passing it by, overlooking it. My belief that Piero usually has something important to tell us has made me look again. This painting is unfinished; it was found in Piero's workshop at his death. The green paint has become black and gives a rather scrubby appearance to the picture. It is an uncomfortable scene—there seems to be no coming together. The

Figure 22.   Piero della Francesca, *The Nativity*
(National Gallery, London).

angels do not seem to be singing the same song. The men are not talking together. One man raises his hand in an authoritarian manner. Mary is rapt in her prayer, far from her baby, and Jesus— unswaddled and unattended to—lies pleading to be picked up. One notices with some relief that he is lying on Mary's cloak— some connection between the two of them. The stable is a bleak and minimal place. The magpie, a bird of dubious character, is perched above the whole scene. This picture reminds me of situations we often have on the NICU: parents who are in reality homeless, often immigrants or refugees, very poor; families struggling under the impact of a new baby, preoccupied with their own thoughts, worries, fantasies, not speaking to each other, or singing different tunes; the baby thrust from the relative security of the watery inside space into the air of this uncontaining new world. In Piero's work all of these elements are held together as a picture, first in the artist's mind and then on the canvas within a frame. Perhaps we have a similar task on the NICU: to hold the babies, the families, and ourselves together first in our minds and then in our work.

Although at first sight these Renaissance pictures of the Madonna and Child impress one with their great beauty, sometimes one notices that the saints standing around are carrying the instruments of their horrible torture. So in Bellini's *Mary with Child and Saints* (Figure 23), we see St Lucy, with her lamp symbolizing her eyes, which had been torn out, being miraculously restored; St Lucy was a determined virgin, who was threatened with death by violation, burning, and the sword. We also see St Catherine, carrying a wheel to remind us that she was broken on a wheel. Another Bellini, *Madonna with Child and Saints* (Figure 24), shows St Sebastian with the arrows sticking in him. I do not think that we would be honest if we denied that the sight of mothers and babies often stirs burning and piercing feelings of envy and pain. We can, of course, quite quickly dismiss these with a rather officious or overly managerial attitude, which is designed to denigrate at least the mother and so lessen our envy. The sight of a mother nursing her baby may arouse all kinds of infantile feelings of our own of being left out. In fact, we know on the NICU that almost nothing stirs the unit up quite so much as the issue of breast-feeding. If we are not able to own these feelings, our eyes may hurt when we look at this

Figure 23.   Giovanni Bellini, *Mary with Child and Saints*
(Church of San Zacharia, Venice).

powerfully intimate scene, and we may then become intrusive,
spoiling, and harmful.

* * *

I would like to illustrate this with a case from the NICU. Mrs
"Green" had come to the unit with her 30-week-old baby boy
twins from another hospital. This is always a disruption and a

Figure 24.   Giovanni Bellini, *Madonna with Child and Saints*
(formerly in the Church of S. Giobbe, Venedi; Galleria dellí
Accademia, Venice).

complication, as the parents have to get used to a new hospital and
new ways of doing things; they also lose contact with staff whom
they may have begun to trust, and they have to put up with the
journey. On the staff's side, they have not experienced the labour
and first few hours that make them feel that this mother and baby
are "theirs". In this case the babies had been conceived by IVF. The

father was quite a great deal older than the mother and had had a previous family. Mother said, rather ruefully, that he found being with someone younger rather embarrassing. She hoped that having the babies would make all of this much better. The staff worried, because father sometimes seemed the worse for drink when he came in at night. Mother was with the twins every day. She looked extremely tired, and it was known that she had to have a kidney biopsy. She was very keen to breast-feed but was having trouble eating well herself. She looked exhausted and made no secret of the fact that she smoked quite heavily. The speech and language therapist, who has a special interest in breast-feeding, was keen to help and introduced the boys to cup-feeding—so that the nurses could cup-feed them when mother was not there. This is felt to be less subversive of the breast-feeding.

Feelings began to run high on the unit about this mother and her babies. Some nurses felt that she was being forced to breast-feed—that it was cruel of the doctors and the speech therapist. One nurse on the ward said how cruel it was and that it was unnecessary; according to another, this nurse only said that because she had not breast-fed her own children. Mother had been on a course of Maxelon, a drug to help her milk supply, and the speech therapist wanted her to have a second course. The doctors were loath to request the GP to prescribe this because it was against the guidelines for Maxelon. Also, there was a question about why her milk was not coming through—was it because she was not eating properly or caring for herself adequately, and should this be treated with medication? The senior registrar and the speech therapist felt undermined by all of this dissension, which it was difficult to get clearly voiced anyway. When mother was asked by several different people whether she wanted to breast-feed, she seemed quite clear that she did. Some nurses pointed out that in any one day mother was not breast-feeding the babies very much, that they were being fed mostly by cup, so they were not even getting the sucking satisfaction from the bottle. The speech therapist felt that the charts did not show accurately how much the mother was feeding them. At this time the unit was very busy, and there was great pressure to take in other babies and particularly not to have to turn away babies that had been born in "our" hospital. Perhaps behind all this was the idea that these babies were not "ours". The senior registrar felt that he was being laughed at by the consultants and staff for his support of the breast-feeding. We tried to air all of these feelings at our weekly meeting. The consultants felt that the babies should really be at home, whereas the speech therapist had set up a programme that involved more time in hospital. Pressure on spaces rose.

Once breast-feeding was quite well established, mother, who had been pushing to go home, was told that she could go. But when it happened, she experienced this as very sudden—perhaps another premature dropping. Twelve hours after they had gone home, she brought them back with the snuffles, and she herself had a sore throat. The senior registrar checked them over and said that they were fine. After a few days the mother gave up breast-feeding. She told the speech therapist that she felt this was connected with such a quick discharge. Some weeks later she refused the invitation to come and talk over all of this. There was some feeling on the unit of not having served this mother well and a resolve to do better in the future. So perhaps we can be aware that while looking at the mother and baby, we carry some hostile feelings—some instruments of torture.

* * *

Any mother in her honest moments will know that she, too, has ambivalent feelings towards her baby, that at times it is not the murderer out there that is to be feared, but the murderer within. This is a very hard fact for us to acknowledge, and it causes many mothers some fear, which can emerge in all kinds of ways. Many new mothers try to split off their murderous feelings onto another object.

* * *

Ms "Edwards", a very successful professional woman, had longed for a baby. She bought a small dog consciously as a trial run, and after the success of this, she eventually got pregnant. During the pregnancy she had many worries about whether she would be able to love the baby, whether she would have any life left of her own. Once the baby was born, full-term and after a reasonable labour, she fell in love with him. Breast-feeding was established and was very successful, and Ms Edwards postponed going back to work.

A few weeks after the birth she took her baby out for a walk in his sling with her cousin and the dog. Her cousin asked how she was, and she said, without thinking, that she was fine but she would like to kick the dog's head in. She was staggered by the vehemence of this and her insight into her own murderous feelings.

* * *

The story of Ms "Finch" was different. Her baby was 31 weeks' gestation but was very small for his dates. The mother had smoked and drunk alcohol throughout her pregnancy and felt very guilty about this. She had an emergency section. A scan showed that the baby had cysts on his brain—the doctors felt that it was hard to make a prognosis but that the outlook could be serious. The mother asked to see me and was very clear that she wanted to meet regularly in a room away from the baby. She told me of her own very painful and difficult life and of how, in her relationship with her husband, this baby had felt like a new start. She struggled hard at understanding her own feelings of guilt, her wish at times to push her husband out, her disappointment and anger at having a baby with problems, her fear of what these problems might be, and the frustration at not knowing what they were facing. At first, this mother had been anxious to return to work—she felt that work held her together. She went to see her boss, who was very reassuring, and she brought home a project to work on. She felt relieved that they had not forgotten her at work and glad that her work persona was intact. However, the baby soon filled her mind, and she no longer wanted to do any work on the project at the moment. The fact that that door was not closed to her seemed to enable her to turn her attention to her son and to value this work and her commitment to him.

To some extent this mother was helped by her baby's obvious need for her. His oxygen levels improved when she picked him up, and he was rooting for the breast, licking it, and resting beside it before he could feed from it. Father, who had avoided me, then came to a meeting and seemed relieved to talk. The baby's progress was so good—he was growing well, his head was growing, he was soon feeding—that the doctors felt that the parents had lost sight of the fact that he might well have considerable problems. When these were mentioned to mother, it was almost as if she had not heard it before. She came and talked it over, saying that it felt so awful; she knew that she had already been told, but she had had a fantasy that when they took him home, everything would be all right. She said that when she was with him, it did not seem so bad; it was when she was at home that she started chewing things over. Supported by the speech therapist, breast-feeding went very well, and the parents soon took the baby home. It seemed that feeding continued well, with the baby making it clear that he liked the breast and not the bottle. The parents were delighted to be at home. But mother said that she worried a lot about how his development would go. In the meantime he was a very demanding baby, wanting to sleep nestled into mother. Mother continued to come for occasional sessions and in these she voiced her fears that her baby would probably be very damaged—unable, she thought, to sit or walk. She told me that she felt she no longer had a life, that she never would have one again, and how much she wished that he had died. With some difficulty but a great sense of relief she told me that when he had had to have a small operation, she had wished that he would die. She spoke enviously of other parents whose premature babies had died. Being allowed to articulate these deathly thoughts seemed to make them more human and to enable her to get on better with her baby.

* * *

A painter who seems to have understood the close interrelation of birth and death, of nurturing and murderousness, is Poussin. He was a French painter in the seventeenth century who loved Italy and who, even when summoned to the French court as Royal painter, soon escaped from it and went to live permanently in Italy. In his painting *The Nurture of Jupiter* (Figure 25), we see the chubby baby Jupiter suckling from a goat. One nymph is collecting honey from the tree and another, a river nymph, pours water into the stream. But the goat's vigorous legs and horns have to be held by a nymph and a satyr. We also notice that there are some bees swarming to the right of the tree; the tree, although it is sprouting new growth, has been stunted, and perhaps the gaze of the *putto* is rather upsettingly intrusive. We read the story: Jupiter's father, Saturn, had eaten his first five sons, and Jupiter's mother had sent her new baby away to be looked after by the nymphs of the moun-

Figure 25.   Nicolas Poussin, *The Nurture of Jupiter*
(Dulwich Art Gallery, London).

tains. It seems that Poussin was able to envisage the fecundity of
nature and human nature as seen in birth, feeding, honey, flowing
water—that is, all the resources we need—as involving an acceptance of our own deathly or destructive side. My argument is that if
we are unable to accept this ambivalence in our nature, we will
find it hard to understand the feelings of some of the people we
may be trying to help.

These mixed feelings that mothers—and fathers—have about
conception, pregnancy, labour, and child-rearing are not helped by
the idealization of these events promoted by our culture. The other
side of this idealization is that the task of mothering is not one that
is highly prized in our culture, where women are expected to

return to work very soon after giving birth. In this atmosphere, where the real work of having babies is not adequately considered, mothers are left horrified by the feelings that they know themselves to have, or else they split them off into other "bad" women and seek to deal with or hate them there. There is more risk of these feelings being acted out when they cannot be acknowledged or worked with. Just as Mary had her mother's lap, mothers in general need a holding environment to help them cope with their often very difficult tasks. A NICU and the various professionals can do something to provide such a lap, but it is likely that we will fail in this unless we recognize our own mixed feelings.

CHAPTER SEVEN

Mourning for a baby

I began to write the paper that this chapter is based on several years ago, while my own father was dying. I was rather slow to realize how ill he was. and it was only with the help of Dr Carter, one of the consultant paediatricians, that I understood that he was close to death. I still imagined that in the summer ahead I would be sitting in the garden chatting to him. I had accompanied him to hospital for treatment and had visited him, believing that he would soon return to his home with my mother. I was scheduled to talk to the paediatricians about mourning on a particular day a week after his admission, and I planned to drive thereafter the 70 miles to where he was in hospital. That morning I had a message from my brother to say that my father was much worse. I asked one of my daughters to cancel my talk to the paediatricians, make various phone-calls for me, and follow me by train. I set off in the pelting rain, arguing with myself as I went: doctors would not have cancelled a talk just like that, I was probably panicking, but on the other hand this was my father, and he was very ill. When I arrived at the hospital, my father was asleep and very cold. In alarm I tried to ring my mother; it turned out that she was on her way. Other members of my family arrived, and we spent the day and night with my father until he died at five o'clock in the morning, fighting against death. In moments of lucidity he had cursed the pain, he had kissed my mother, struggling to get past the oxygen mask, and telling her that it, their life together, had been wonderful. At one point, as I tried to help him to the toilet, which he insisted on struggling to, he told me that he was very ill, and then his insides seemed to run out of him.

I stayed with my mother for the next few days while family and friends gathered for the funeral. In that time I had this dream:

> *I was driving to my hometown to read my paper to the paediatricians. I stopped in the High Street at my father's old shop—a place full of familiarity and significance to me. But the door was locked, and the blind was down. Sadly I turned back to my car, but now this was locked too. I worried about whether my paper was inside the car, but I set off on foot through the familiar town, to the Assembly Rooms, where I was to read my paper.* [As a small girl I had learnt ballet dancing there from an intriguing woman who had red painted nails. She had been a childhood friend of my father's, and he would tell stories of her doing wonderful cartwheels.] *In the Assembly Rooms I noticed that neither Dr Carter nor Dr Kennedy were there—I wondered how I could speak without a friendly ear to listen. Someone told me that Dr Kennedy could not be there because she had had to go to see her sister, who was in some trouble, but that she had left me a file. I rummaged through this, hoping to find my paper, but all I could find was a black hat. Then I noticed that my old friend and colleague, Dr Gibbons, was in the audience. Cheered, I sat at the table and saw my folder there, but when I opened it to speak, I found that the paper was by him, not by me.*

The sense of closure in this dream seemed characteristic of mourning; to find the shop, which I had always found open and welcoming to me, closed, was devastating. I also found myself thrust back into old dear memories, and perhaps a sense of my father's having had a life that I did not know about. The entry of this painted woman, whom consciously I liked, suggests some more spiteful or murderous feelings on my part. In the dream I was very dependent on good supportive figures, and these seemed temporarily to have deserted me. I was cut off from confidence in my own creativity. Perhaps I was helped by Dr Kennedy putting her family first and reminding me with the black hat to get on with the task of mourning. But the black hat is also the symbol of condemnation by the judge and perhaps in some way I felt guilty of causing my father's death.

I am conscious of two reasons for including this story here. One is as a way of thanking my father for his love, his sense of humour, and his unfailing common sense, which I use as well as I am able in my work. Also, this is a chapter on mourning, and I am aware that what is happening to us in our lives has an influence on our work, however much we may try to hide this. I also know of the impact of dying and dead babies on the staff: of their grief—I see nurses and doctors weeping—and their sense of impotence—I see professionals worrying about how they might do better. There is a pull at such times to quarrel, because this seems like a relief from pain. I know that all of this interacts with the losses in our own personal lives. At the end of one staff support meeting a nurse told us that she had had three children who had died. Dr Gibbons and I were so stunned that we hardly took this news in and offered no sympathy. We still wonder if we heard right.

Macbeth

> What, man! Ne'er pull your hat upon your brows;
> Give sorrow words, the grief that does not speak
> Whispers the o'er fraught heart, and bids it break.
>> Shakespeare, *Macbeth*, Act IV, Scene 3

My attention was drawn to this quotation by Dorothy Judd's wonderful book, *Give Sorrow Words*, which is about a child dying of cancer. It made me think again about Macbeth. This is Malcolm's speech to Macduff, who has just learnt from Rosse that his castle has been surprised and his wife and children killed on the orders of Macbeth. Shakespeare's idea seems to be that grief, if not articulated, works away at the heart and breaks it. Freud, early on, described psychoanalysis as the talking cure—and it continues to be the psychoanalytic belief that the work of giving words to our feelings is a curative one. Poets are able to reach within themselves and to articulate feelings fashioned into verse; we often think that they achieve this with the help of their muse. But most people need the presence of an external person to give voice to their feelings— someone who is at least trying to understand. Sometimes it is the listening person who can help in articulating these unbearable feelings. This task takes us back to our infantile experience, when in benign circumstances those caring for us help us to recognize and name feelings and in this way to have some purchase on them.

This chapter is about my experience with mothers, and sometimes fathers, whose babies have died. I have chosen not to use the word "bereavement" because I think that that word has become worn out—a word that enables us to talk about "cases" without them impinging too greatly on us. I prefer to talk about mourning or, perhaps, heartbreak, because I think that this is what we are dealing with. In fact, as we once saw on the NICU, where care was to be withdrawn from a dying baby and the mother was not heartbroken, the staff experienced a range of very difficult feelings. When a child dies, we feel that it is natural for the mother to be heartbroken. Much of my work is a mutual endeavour with the mother to give this sorrow words.

It may seem odd that I have quoted from *Macbeth*. On the surface it is not much to do with our subject. I was thinking about it because of the power of this particular quotation, and gradually it seemed to me that aspects of it were relevant to us. In this play Shakespeare offers us representations of common irrational fears and wishes, which we ordinarily express in magical and superstitious ways. If we think of the characters as standing for different kinds of thoughts that we all have at times, it becomes a domestic tale and not removed from us.

The story opens with the three witches gathering together on the blasted heath: the atmosphere of magic and menace is set. We learn that in the battle that has just been fought, Macbeth has shown particular bravery and is held dear by his King, Duncan, who plans to reward him. He is popular and highly regarded. The witches appear to Macbeth and to his friend, Banquo, prophesying this reward and finally the crown for Macbeth, but promising to Banquo that his sons shall gain the crown later. It seems that the witches' prophecy activates Macbeth's ambition and greed, and that this is matched by his wife's when he tells her of "this strange business". Together they plan to hurry the prophecy along by murdering the King. The Macbeths have trouble carrying out their plan—Macbeth is particularly plagued by fears and foreboding. Lady Macbeth seems the harder partner. She mocks him for his faintheartedness:

> I have given suck, and know
> How tender 'tis to love the babe that milks me.
> I would, while it was smiling in my face,
> Have plucked my nipple from his boneless gums,
> And dashed the brains out, had I so sworn
> As you have done to this!

Shakespeare, Macbeth, Act I, Scene 7

The murderous conspiracy is enacted, and the Macbeths dig themselves further and further into their plans, so that there seems no way out for them. Lady Macbeth can no longer speak to her husband: her mind cracks, and she goes mad. He is plagued by thoughts and tries to blot them out, plunging himself into more and more bloody deeds. He cannot bear that Banquo's child should eventually gain the crown, so he murders Banquo and tries to murder his son, Fleance. As part of Macbeth's reign of terror, Lady Macduff, portrayed as a motherly figure, is murdered with her children.

* * *

Shakespeare acknowledges the power of superstitious thoughts to motivate our fears and our ambition. We learn of the cruelty towards babies that can overtake us, and of how difficult it can be to extricate ourselves from these states of mind. These emotions are within us all—under a thin veneer of rationality. I think that the death of a baby is such a dreadful thing that this veneer is ripped away and we are confronted by terrifying thoughts. We have become familiar in Accident and Emergency with how parents of a child who has died can hound the doctors and nurses involved; how an atmosphere of blame can rule. Sometimes the parents feel that they are to blame for what has happened to their child and project that onto the medical staff, who also have to cope with their own feelings of guilt. In staff support meetings we learn how disastrous this can be for professional people's lives, leading good doctors and nurses to be wracked with tormenting fears and to contemplate giving up work. We now have a culture that quickly takes these things to court, and the feelings of guilt mushroom. The media seem to batten off such stories, waylaying nurses leaving the hospital after long shifts, trying to extract gory stories from them. This is unfortunate, because it gets in the way of the hard work of mourning and exploits the mad and paranoid feelings we all have around the death of a child.

In talking to mothers whose babies have died, I have been struck by how frequently they report, with embarrassment, thoughts about magic, about curses, about evil spirits who have taken the baby away, about prophetic dreams before the death, about murderous thoughts towards their baby, which, they feel, involve them in guilty complicity in its death. I think that such thoughts float in and out of all our minds, and at times of stress we can become fixated on them and superstitious. Because these thoughts are not very acceptable to our modern, scientific, daylit minds, mothers are often left with no relief from them. As for Lady Macbeth, we might think that she does not present a very pretty example of motherhood—and yet we are told of a softer, gentler side of her. One of the mysteries of the play is: where, indeed, are Lady Macbeth's children?

If we examine our own feelings about babies and listen very carefully to our patients, we realize that our love is mixed in with quite a lot of hatred. Most mourning mothers that I have listened to have, at some level, felt that they have caused their baby's death— that bursts of irritation, fleeting moments of hatred, of wishing him dead, of considering an abortion, and so on, are remembered with pain and secretly believed to be the cause of death. One question is, can this be shared with anyone as human, or does the mother have to carry this locked in her heart? Lady Macbeth goes mad from her sense of guilt and remorse, and many mothers I have seen have been afraid that they are going mad because of the kinds of thoughts they are having. The hope is that thinking and talking about these feelings show them to be more normal. In emphasizing these darker feelings, I do not want to minimize the other feelings—the love, the grief, the loss—but these are usually more obvious and acceptable, even if unbearable.

I have written below about two women whose babies died in very different circumstances. I am not sure why I have chosen to concentrate on my work and relationships with these two women. Thinking of all the parents I have seen in mourning, I realize what protective and strong feelings I have had towards them. It is true that these two women had a very strong impact on me. I once heard a consultant paediatrician say to some junior doctors that one cannot do this kind of work well without being scarred—that if you are unaffected, you know that you are not doing it properly. I think that this is crucial. For the task of listening and bearing the impact of what is said to be authentic, it has to transform the listener as well as the speaker.

* * *

Mrs "Evans" came to me not directly from the NICU but from Dr Carter, a consultant paediatrician based in the NICU, who saw her in Accident and Emergency. He asked me to contact her as part of my work with mothers and babies. It was clear to me that he wanted me to see her partly because he thought that this might be helpful to her but also because of how upset he was.

Child psychotherapists attach great importance to seeing a patient regularly—same time, same place. The aim is to provide a safe, regular environment that enables the patient to unravel her feelings—and where her feelings towards the therapist can be explored, when this is helpful, without the therapist's own experience, moods, and anxieties being thrust onto the patient. It is very difficult to achieve this in a hospital environment, but my work with Mrs Evans was nearer to that model than usual, largely due to her commitment and concentration. I first saw her in paediatric out-patients, on a Friday evening, so that she would not have to see the children in the out-patient clinic. The following week we arrived at the door together and found it locked. We went to the NICU, which was in temporary accommodation, and when she saw the cots in the far distance, she went white and seemed to be stuck to the door. We took refuge in a small, cluttered store-room. She managed this for another week. Then I asked the hospital chaplain if I could borrow his office, next to the chapel. She was happier with that and ignored the exuberant and joyful organ practice when she was telling me of particularly painful feelings. One week we were locked out and took refuge in the chapel itself. I was grateful to have it but was worried about whether she would be inhibited in her exploration of unacceptable feelings by being in a holy place. It turned out to be more my difficulty than hers. She was there to work.

Mrs Evans came every week for a year and a half, except for holidays. She was always on time, and we met for 55 minutes. Her capacity to hold on to the work, to throw herself into the enterprise, was remarkable. She recounted to me many times the events of the day "Zoe" died, each time telling me a little more or from a different point of view. A new piece of information required a re-telling of the story.

She had decided to go back to work when Zoe was 4 months old, and Zoe's grandmother was going to look after her. But it emerged that Zoe was not only a very active baby, but also very colicky and hard to comfort. Mrs Evans was worried that she might be too much for her mother, and when she suggested this, her mother was very relieved. Grandmother looked after Zoe for three weeks while some other arrangements could be made. Grandmother had a best friend, whose daughter—also a friend of Mrs Evans—was a child-minder. She agreed to look after Zoe when mother went to work. She knew Zoe and had come to the house several times. So the new arrangement was to start in Mrs Evans's fourth week back at work. Monday was a Bank Holiday, and on Tuesday Zoe was taken to the child-minder. That evening, Zoe was quiet and looked sad. Mrs Evans remembered it well. She re-marked to her husband that Zoe looked so sad that she felt sorry for her. She went to the child-minder on Wednesday and Thursday, and then again on Friday. On the Friday Zoe had only been there for one hour, asleep, when the child-minder found her dead and rushed her to hospital. Mrs Evans was called at work and told to go to Casualty. She said that she knew immediately that Zoe was dead. She rushed there and sat with her in her arms. She did not want to put her down. After some hours, her husband persuaded her to go home, and she did, but returned in the evening. She hated leaving Zoe and asked the kind woman at the undertakers to put the heat up to keep Zoe warm. It is hard for me to convey how Mrs Evans recounted this story and worked over it, elaborating it.

One week she told me about how, a few days before Zoe died, she had had a nightmare that an evil spirit was rattling on the window, trying to get in, that it wanted to take Zoe away, and that she had awoken in terror. She was clearly embarrassed and frightened telling me about this—wondering whether I would think she was mad, whether there were evil spirits, and, lying outside this thought, terrible questions about where Zoe was now—whether she was in some evil place, or abandoned in the cold earth, or whether she was in some way safe in her mother's mind, where she could talk to her. I noticed how Mrs Evans veered around in her thoughts and feelings, and she was aware of this too. Sometimes it frightened her. She wondered whether she was unstable, whether she was going mad. She soon realized that I could not give her any answers, but she was reassured that I valued all these thoughts and feelings, recognizing that this was the hard work of mourning and not surprised that she was exhausted. I did point out to her that it would be very strange if she were not in pain, and that her tears and feelings were very precious. This seemed to make her feel less persecuted by them. She said that she was doing very little at home, but she felt she had no time to do anything, she was so preoccupied.

Again and again Mrs Evans reiterated that no one was to blame. But she kept coming back to the question of why it had happened. This ran like a thread throughout our meetings. She constantly beat her head against the question: what had caused Zoe's death . . . she and her husband had done nothing wrong . . . they would be the same with another baby . . . how could they know the same thing would not happen with another baby? Sometimes her face softened with thoughts of Zoe, and even with the hope of another baby; sometimes it hardened in bitterness, driving away all soft and tender thoughts.

When she was angry, Mrs Evans chewed round the same thoughts: Why did the doctors not know, why did the government not give more money for cot death research? She felt persecuted by the media coverage of cot death research. And then, more desperately, she wondered why her baby had died at the child-minder's, why she had been put to sleep upstairs, thinking sadly that Zoe had never slept away from them. Mother was terrified that Zoe had woken in a panic and died. It was most unbearable to her that she was not there with her when she had died, had not been there

with her, in whatever state she was in. And the thought of her
dying alone was dreadful. I think that it was in her mind that her
little girl had died of a broken heart not to be with her mother. She
told me that she had wanted to see her friend, the child-minder, on
the Sunday before she began babysitting, to tell her all the little
things about Zoe—what she liked and what she did not. Mrs
Evans went up to the child-minder's house, but she was busy with
her own children, and there had not been a moment. Then, on
Tuesday morning, Mrs Evans thought she would tell the child-
minder when she came to collect Zoe—but she was late and her
own mother shooed her out of the house, telling her that she could
manage and Mrs Evans should go to work. So she went, and in the
late afternoon her husband collected Zoe. This was the pattern on
Wednesday and Thursday—and she never did have her talk with
the child-minder. I think this weighed on her mind—that there
never was a proper hand-over.

Sometimes Mrs Evans's feelings erupted in another way—not
towards blaming herself, but towards blaming the child-minder.
She blamed her for putting Zoe upstairs, for putting her to sleep on
her side, for, as it emerged, sending her child up to see if Zoe was
awake. And these thoughts could teeter over into the unthink-
able—that she was murdered. This was exacerbated by the police
coming to Mrs Evans's house on the day Zoe died to get details
about the child-minder and going there to investigate. In her mind,
they burst in, although they may have come quite tactfully as part
of standard police practice when a child has died. These thoughts
of murder reappeared from time to time—with the feeling that
that way madness lay. I think that it was a tremendous relief to her
that I could hear this calmly without getting caught up and overwhelmed myself. Gradually she was able to talk more openly of
her hatred—her hatred of the child-minder and of the whole
world. Sometimes she felt that it was she and Zoe against the
whole world. And I think she often held on to her hatred with grim
determination, because it was not so unbearable as the days when
she was overwhelmed by the loss.

The absence of her baby in her arms, the emptiness, the si-
lence—these she described with the utmost poignancy. She said
that she could tell me, because I did not cry, like her husband and

her mother; she did not have to worry about her own crying, as she did with them. On the other hand, unlike the rest of the world, I would listen, and I seemed to understand. I knew that I was helped by my training to listen, to reflect, and to bear what I was hearing—but I also knew that what she told me had a tremendous impact on me, and I think she had some sense of that and was relieved that she could touch me so particularly. She told me that every night she went to sleep holding Zoe's blanket—it still smelt of her—and that Zoe's smell pervaded the house. She dreaded this wearing off. The imprint of her head was still in her cot. She dreaded the days since death outnumbering the days of her life. I could feel her yearning for Zoe's physical presence. I think the intensity of this pain also made her worry about whether she would go mad and whether the pain would become so bad that she would not be able to bear it. Again she would slip into blaming everyone else—and this heralded her telling me that she had not breast-fed Zoe—she had not wanted to, and now she felt so bad because she felt that that might have made all the difference.

Throughout all of this Mrs Evans's own mother appeared as a good, supportive figure. I felt that her capacity to use me so trustingly was based on her good experience of her own mother. She was adamant that she did not blame her mother for not feeling strong enough to look after Zoe, and it was hard for her to address her anger with her mother. Her mother was clearly upset and told Mrs Evans that if she had another baby, she would definitely look after it when she went back to work. I pointed out to her from time to time various deficiencies of my own: that I could not tell her why Zoe had died, that I could not say it would not happen again, that I did not make the pain go away, I did not tell her what to do, I would leave her for a week without a session over the New Year. Mrs Evans would grin ruefully and in some way appreciate the truth of these comments.

Mrs Evans's own story with her husband, who was twelve or so years older, turned out to be complicated. He had two daughters from a previous marriage, and his first wife had died. Mrs Evans was only 21 when she had come into his life, and he had hit hard times, being unemployed and drinking heavily. She had pulled him out of this and had moved in, but his mother and sister had always stood in the way of her taking on a mothering role to the two girls. Finally she gave up trying, and what had evolved was a rather distant relationship with them. She had eventually married Mr Evans, but he had not wanted more children. She felt cheated by this but had accepted it. It was only after eight years that she had become pregnant, and then she had wondered whether to have an abortion. She remembered having had unwelcoming feelings to the new baby inside her. But she had decided to have the baby; she had had a good pregnancy but a very hard labour, and she had to be induced. She said that it had taken her a little while to "bond" with Zoe. If Zoe had lived, these different thoughts and feelings would have been more acceptable with the reassurance of a healthy, live baby and her daily care of her. But under the impact of her death, they have all been up for examination. The fact that she could have entertained the idea of killing her baby by abortion was awful to her. She believed that the thoughts you have when you are pregnant affect the baby—so she wondered how these thoughts had affected Zoe. Together we questioned her understandable but real refusal to mother the two girls—who had been very small when they had lost their mother—and wondered about her feelings towards these girls now. With a less idealized, more honest idea of conception, pregnancy, labour, motherhood, Mrs Evans was drawing closer to the two girls. She smiled ironically at how different the reality was from the picture popularly given of motherhood. And in giving up the idealized, bloodless, inhuman view, she was able to acknowledge the murderous, unmotherly, hating, blaming, dark side of herself without fearing that it would obliterate the love, the tenderness, the service, the devotion, and the passion.

After Christmas, although now with more positive thoughts about having another baby, Mrs Evans's mood seemed to become darker. She would remember Zoe with pleasure, telling me all kinds of incidents about her. Zoe appeared in many sessions as a very lively, loveable baby, but Mrs Evans seemed to settle more into bitterness. I felt that there was a battle in her between more optimistic, lively thoughts and a bitter turning away from life. She told me that she was having very frightening nightmares and that she had gone to her GP, who had given her antidepressants, saying that she would advise counselling, but the GP knew that she was seeing me, and that it did not seem to be helping her. Noting to myself that possibly mother's anger and frustration with me was being put into the GP, I asked her about the nightmares. She said that they were always about Zoe: in one *she had got Zoe back from the hospital—she needed feeding, so she had gone to get her bottle, and Zoe had said "please"*. In the dream *she had said to her husband: "They've even taught her to speak"—she had missed that—they had taken even that away. And Zoe was not right, she did not look right. She was handicapped. Later in the dream, whenever she looked at Zoe, she was missing an arm or a leg or some part of her.* She thought she had dreamt this because she had watched a film about Bosnia, where some children, who were starving, had stolen some food and had had their hands cut off. In other dreams *she had not changed Zoe's nappy for three days.* It seemed to me that in these dreams she felt she was not looking after Zoe properly and that she was starving. She agreed and went off into a bitter tirade about her loss: this should not have happened. She had not done anything wrong; other people did all kinds of dreadful things, and it did not happen to them—there was no justice. She would like to turn away from the world and never have another baby.

Gradually Mrs Evans told me how she sometimes made herself go through painful memories, like a torture. I asked her what was happening between her and her mother. I wondered what had happened to her own internal mother, who might protect her from this kind of torture. It emerged that she and her mother, always so close, had recently become estranged, and that her mother was in some pain about this. I wondered whether she was trying to show her mother in some small way what it felt like to lose a daughter. I also thought that there was a feeling that if she could not have a daughter, then her mother should not have one either and would be punished likewise. She said that she would not hurt her mother for the world, she loved her, but she did want someone to know how it felt to be alone with all of this. She then told me how she wished she had held Zoe before the funeral, but she could not— she was frightened. She said she had been a coward. I thought that she was frightened of Zoe because she was dead. She nodded and said that Zoe looked dreadful, not like herself, and she felt so frightened of her. The full impact of this mother's terror in the presence of her dead baby hit me. I remembered Zoe in the dream not looking right. I said that I thought there was a little girl part of Mrs Evans that was frightened in the night with these dreadful dreams, and she wanted to call a good comforting mother who would make some sense of them, as children do in the night. But it seemed as if she was delivered up to a bad witch, who told her when she was so frightened that she was bad, not good enough to be a mother. She told me that she woke from these dreams in great distress, sobbing.

As I spoke more clearly to Mrs Evans about an infantile part of herself, I realized that we were into a new part of our work to-gether—and, indeed, the following week brought much more clearly infantile material. I had started work focused on Zoe's death but then realized that central to the mourning work were Mrs Evans's own unconscious infantile fantasies. Mrs Evans came saying that she had had a better week, but what she described was a grim picture inside her and at home. The atmosphere seemed dominated by a kind of cruelty, epitomized by the story of the starving children stealing bread and having their hands cut off. Her husband was saying that he did not want another child now. Mrs Evans was filled with terror—maybe she would never have another baby—and she thought that she had better not tell him how much she wanted one, because he might continue to refuse. This is what he had done after they were married. And he, his mother, and his sister had all barred her from becoming mother to the girls. I thought there was a little girl part of her that wanted to be a better mummy than her mummy. This little girl wanted to take over mummy's babies and was terrified that she would be punished by not being allowed to have babies. And I wondered if her decision not to breast-feed really stemmed from a belief that she was a little girl and could not be a real mother. She responded to this by telling me that she had had a dream that *Chris, the oldest girl who was 17, had said to her that she, Chris, would be a much better mother than Mrs Evans had been and that Mrs Evans had hated her for that and had thought rather cruelly that Chris would learn.* So there was a fantasy of a cruel mother who would not be able to accept the little girl's competitive, perhaps envious, feelings towards her, but who responded by inflicting some horrible punishment on the lit-tle girl (her hands will be chopped off, she will have no milk, her baby will die and so on). This seemed to make sense of the feelings of terror. I remembered the child-minder's daughter, who had found Zoe dead, and I wondered what sort of state she was in now. Mrs Evans had refused to have any sympathy or anxiety for her. When I asked, she told me that the girl was only 13 and that she had become so upset that they had had to change the house around and throw out things that Zoe had used. This made Mrs Evans hate the whole family. It was hard for this hatred to be alleviated, because the child-minder refused to see her and talk to her, which made Mrs Evans feel shut out from the last few hours of her daughter's life.

Mrs Evans then told me that the reason why the child-minder could not talk to her on that Sunday before she began to look after Zoe was because her older daughter, who had caused her a lot of "grief" and who had been in trouble with the police, was moving out to her dad's. The child-minder was very upset. Mrs Evans told her to let her daughter go, she would soon be pleased to come back. It seemed that on that Sunday in some way the child-minder had lost her daughter.

At this time Mrs Evans felt that she was destined not to be a mother, that she never would be, that her husband did not want her to have a baby. So she might well leave the whole pack of them. He was in an alliance with his daughters anyway. I felt that she had succumbed to her infantile fantasy that a withholding father did not want her to have a baby, and that she would be punished by a cruel mother for wanting to compete with her or to steal her babies. And in this mood she became this punishing mother to the girls.

As I got into this kind of material with Mrs Evans, I wondered how she would respond to it, but it seemed to make sense to her, and she was gradually able to think more about having another baby and to talk to her husband about this.

* * *

What I want to emphasize is that in a mother's mourning work for her dead baby there will inevitably be an admixture of her own unconscious baby feelings towards her own mother and father. With Mrs Evans, there was the adult work of mourning for her baby and experiencing the loss—but there was also a terrified child, whose rather normal infantile fantasies of competition and punishment had been seemingly confirmed by the reality of her baby dying. It was no good just saying to her that she was not to blame. Of course she was not to blame, and her rational logical self might know that she was not to blame, but her irrational magical baby self believed that she was to blame and that she should be punished and could be punished, and this had to be addressed. Reassurance can be damaging, in that it can prevent us from attending to our deeper feelings, and it can also make us feel desperate that nobody else understands that what we fear is true.

* * *

The situation of the second mother was rather different: while Mrs Evans had a lovely, healthy baby who died unexpectedly at 5 months, Mrs "Abdullah" had a baby who was born very damaged. "Sami" was her first baby, and he was born with multiple abnormalities, which added up to a particular syndrome. He had difficulty breathing, and he was small and ugly. He could not feed normally and had to have a gastrostomy, a drain to the oesophagus, into his neck. He had problems with his liver and kidneys. He had recurrent chest infections and fits. His head did not grow, and he was deaf. Dr Carter asked me to see the parents.

I saw them with Sami on the Children's Ward several times. I did not feel that I had made very good contact with them. Father spoke very little English. Mother was busy looking after Sami and was distressed by his condition. She cared for him devotedly but perhaps rather roughly. Eventually he went home, but his parents often had to bring him back to hospital. The speech therapist told me that mother would like to see me, and I went to visit her at home. We sat very formally in a cold, bare room, and she poured out her worries. I arranged to meet her the following week. Then, quite suddenly, mother brought Sami to the hospital. He deteriorated over a few days and died. I rang the parents, and there was no answer. I knocked at the door, and there was nobody at home. I wondered anyway how I would fit into their Muslim mourning rites. I wrote to Mrs Abdullah and said that I would call at a particular time—and she was there. We then met every week for several weeks. We would sit rather formally side by side, and mother would talk. She talked about the emptiness—and her terrible fear of the emptiness. She was afraid to be in the house on her own—as soon as I left, she would go back to her mother's. She could not go downstairs to the toilet on her own, her husband had to go with her. She had nothing any more—she missed Sami, he was hers. She even missed the hospital. Everything was so quiet, and she had nothing to do. Sami had suffered so much, it was dreadful to witness. Many people felt that it was better that he had died, but she and her husband could not feel that—he was their son. She hated all those who said that it was better. She wanted him, no matter how he was.

She told me that she had become pregnant when Sami was a few months old; on the scan this baby was seen to be very abnormal, so she had had an abortion at 19 weeks of gestation. This was several weeks before Sami died. She felt very guilty about this and condemned by her religion, but she felt that she could not have coped with this baby while caring for Sami.

She told me that she thought that someone had put a curse on her—someone back home in Pakistan. It turned out that this was the third time she was married: one husband had left her, and one was impotent. Now she felt sure that her husband's family would turn against her. They would want him to leave her and go back home. In the face of all these fears, she and her husband were not speaking to each other. Things were very bad between them. He went out every day, looking for work. She would have liked to have another baby, but he said no—never.

This outpouring would go on every week, and every time I left after an hour, she would say she did not know how I could bear to hear it.

Mrs Abdullah also talked about how she hated other children. She felt emotionally cut off from her nephews and nieces. She was horrified at the strength and violence of her own feelings. She felt estranged from her own family and could not bear to go to family gatherings.

She also talked about blaming the hospital for Sami's death. She had brought him up to Casualty on Monday evening, and they had been sent home without treatment. He was very ill. On Tuesday morning he seemed strange, and she fell asleep. When she woke up, he was unconscious; he never regained consciousness.

Beneath her blame of the hospital was her blame of herself. She often seemed to gain some strength from blaming others and from her hatred.

Gradually things seemed to ease. One week her little niece was at the house to keep her company. Then it seemed that she and her husband were on talking terms and that he might in the future be prepared to try again. Then his family were pressing them both to come to Pakistan for a holiday. Gradually I realized that this holiday was to include a visit to Mecca, to pray for better things and to allay the curse. One week Mrs Abdullah asked me to come to her mother's house for the next session—it would not be much further for me to cycle! I found my way there, and Mrs Abdullah's brother came to the door. There was a lot of calling out in a busy household, and Mrs Abdullah emerged, smiling. She had forgotten me and was praying—but I should come in. We sat and talked, and wonderful food appeared, prepared by grandmother in the kitchen. I realized that Mrs Abdullah was back in the heart of her family. She was excited to be going to Pakistan. She felt deeply the loss of Sami, but she felt that he had suffered enough pain. She said that I should ring her again when she got back from Pakistan in the new year.

Postscript

Both Mrs Evans and Mrs Abdullah got pregnant again, and they gave birth within a fortnight of each other. I saw them both throughout their pregnancies and listened to all their hopes and terrible fears, and to the feelings of guilt towards the dead child for having another baby.

Mrs Evans had another little girl. The labour was much easier, and the baby, "Miranda", was well. Mrs Evans had cracked nipples and did not manage to breast-feed, but she enjoyed this baby in a way she had not believed she would be able to. However, she could not leave her with anyone else, so it was hard at first for her husband or her mother to relate to her. Miranda was very content and happy, and Mrs Evans found the contrast with Zoe, who had been so difficult to comfort, quite painful. Over several years I have seen Miranda grow into a very determined and loveable girl, who talks quite openly about her sister, Zoe. I continue to see Mrs Evans occasionally.

Mrs Abdullah also had a little girl. She was found to have a central cleft palate. Mother took her home but brought her back after she had had a fit. She stayed in the NICU for a week, and during this time mother was very distressed, feeling that once again she had a damaged baby. However, she took her home, bearing enormous levels of anxiety. The medical staff found it hard to view this little girl except in terms of her brother, and their levels of anxiety were very high too. It was unclear what difficulties she had, if any, apart from the cleft palate. Over time it turned out that she did have some other disabilities, and she had to attend a special school.

Mrs Abdullah went on to have another child—this time, a healthy son.

> Grief fills the room up of my absent child,
> Lies in his bed, walks up and down with me,
> Puts on his pretty looks, repeats his words,
> Remembers me of all his gracious parts,
> Stuffs out his vacant garments with his form:
> Then I have reason to be fond of grief.
>
> Shakespeare, *King John*, Act III, Scene 4

Note

I would like to thank both of these women for sharing their lives so intimately with me. I would also like to thank the many other women who have talked to me so openly and poignantly about their children who have died.

CHAPTER EIGHT

The web

O! let him pass; he hates him
That would upon the rack of this tough world
Stretch him out longer.

Shakespeare, *King Lear*, Act V, Scene 3

In *Middlemarch*, George Eliot writes: "I . . . have so much to do in unravelling certain human lots, and seeing how they were woven and interwoven, that all the light that I can command must be concentrated on this particular web, and not dispersed over that tempting range of relevancies called the universe." It seems that in this she was influenced by the seventeenth-century philosopher, Spinoza, whose work she was translating in 1885–86. Spinoza elaborated a very complicated metaphysical theory in which he argued for the interconnectedness of everything and for the view that in saying anything about the world, we necessarily say something false in that what we say can only be part of the story. This is a very compelling idea, and in the foregoing quotation George Eliot was, I think, struggling with it. She wanted to think about her characters in depth, she placed them in their families and social context, and in *Middlemarch* she gave some political

145

and social background, but she was aware that there are all kinds of "relevancies" that she did not consider.

I often think about work in the NICU in these terms. I find myself putting the babies at the centre of the web. Each one is very complicated—we need to think about them, mind and body. In our weekly unit meeting we try to think about their relations with their mothers, to place them in their families, to think about the families' social situations and their emotional states. At this point the web opens out, and we soon realize that the "relevancies" are infinite. The story of one particular family often seems crucially relevant to the prematurity of the baby. Often there have been deaths in the family or losses of other kinds. Families may be immigrants or refugees, or they may suffer from chronic poverty, and immediately we are into political issues. As if this were not enough, we find that these families, who are now on the unit, have an effect on each other—and not only that, but also on us, and we on them.

So another vein of relevancy opens: the effect of the babies and families on us and on those with whom we live. As I have described unit life, this may seem rather peripheral—the babies are naturally at the centre and the staff on the edge, but in this interconnectedness we can turn our attention to any part; so long as we are not too daunted by all that we are not looking at, we can think about particular aspects. It is with the place of the staff in this web that I am concerned in this chapter: I want to recast my picture of that place and then give two vignettes of work on the unit.

In talking about the staff's position, I feel driven to go back to talk about the babies. We may not all have babies, but we have all been babies, and we all know, deeply, what babies need. They need to be held, fed, cleaned, thought about, talked to, worried about, loved—and all this preferably by their mothers and fathers. They need to know that they can have some impact, that an urgent cry brings some response, that a gurgle is sometimes noticed. We all have nightmares at times of a very primitive kind of falling, of dissolving, of losing our skin, and then, perhaps more sophisticatedly, of not being able to get away from our persecutors. These states are sometimes described in poetry. The Psalmist says of a moment of terror: "I am poured out like water, and all my bones are out of joint: my heart is like wax; it is melted in the midst of my bowels"' (Psalm 22, *The Book of Common Prayer*). In the face of this, we realize that a NICU is a nightmare—by which I am not saying that it should not exist, or that it is bad, but I do believe that all those working there experience it as a nightmare and that we hide this from ourselves. The unit becomes ordinary life, the norm, babies outside look big: one can even feel rather critical of them— they look monstrous, as if these little mites were better.

I think the situation of the babies—not being held by their mothers, not enjoying feeding, enduring painful procedures—has an enormous effect on doctors and nurses. Junior doctors become upset by procedures they have to perform on babies, nurses become angry and irritable when they are not able to make a baby comfortable. The whole enterprise of the unit is to save life, to present the mother with a baby—a mother who may be in despair about her ability to have a baby. The motives of the staff may be very reparative, the wish to help, to make things all right, but they have to tolerate a lot of pain to do this and to tolerate nagging questions that sometimes surface. These questions can either be suppressed or, with a lot of courage, we can face them as a community.

Members of staff not only have to face the unnatural and sometimes painful situation of the babies, they also have to witness the pain of the mothers and the fathers. The mothers are often very grateful to the unit—they think that it is a wonderful place, that everyone is so helpful, that the baby could not be in better hands— but staff know that there is always another story: that the parents are devastated to find themselves with their baby on the unit, that they feel deprived of being able to care for their babies themselves, that this is not at all how they had imagined things would be, that they can feel quite angry with the nurses because they take over their babies. Sometimes staff can sympathize with this, at other times they snap and feel like retorting that if it were not for them, the mothers would not have a baby at all.

Perhaps every new mother feels somehow that she is usurping her own mother's place, that she is just a little girl pretending to be the mother. A healthy baby helps her to become a mother. She feels that she has produced a baby and that now she can look after it. Having a premature baby can make her feel incompetent (doctors talk about an incompetent cervix.) She may feel that she has dropped the baby, that she cannot be a mother. Many mothers feel that they are being punished for some wrong, and this wrong usually turns out to be what she feels are attacks on a baby: a previous termination, or thoughts about a termination, or ambivalent feelings about this baby. Most women have mixed feelings about their babies, but they are reassured that their aggressive feelings have not been damaging by the presence of a lively, healthy baby. But mothers with sick babies often feel confirmed in their view that they have been destructive to their babies.

Fathers, too, often feel more useless on the unit than they would at home, where they would have the privacy to find their new place, which requires a sensitive and tricky adjustment. The staff have a difficult job in welcoming fathers—even the idea of welcoming emphasizes the fact that this is not the family's own home.

In our unit many of the parents have crippling social problems: there are parents who are very poor, badly housed, out of work; mothers who are looking after children on their own; families that are immigrants or refugees, far from their own families. Staff are often upset by these circumstances and wish to rescue the families. Then there are mothers who are on drugs, whose babies are born addicted. This can arouse all kinds of feelings in the staff—for instance, anger with the mother: how can she have inflicted this on her baby? Other staff feel sorry for her and sometimes feel foolish when they believe stories of reform, which, they discover, are not true. Some mothers are prostitutes, and there may be worries about what kinds of lives the babies are going to have. Sometimes the father is the mother's pimp, and there have been cases on the unit where he is hustling the mother to get back to work. Sometimes the violence around these families is very great, and there may be a real fear for the mother's life. Sometimes we have a mother in from the local women's prison, and the unit has to accommodate the presence of two wardens whenever the mother is there. These sorts of situations cause many difficult feelings: curiosity, voyeurism, horror, a sense of superiority, condemnation, and so on. At times the staff feel in physical danger themselves. Some parents may have unusual life styles with more than one partner, or the identity of the father may be unclear, or they may be a homosexual couple. Whether or not it is politically correct, we are dishonest if we deny that this arouses all kinds of feelings in us. We may have a sophisticated view of how we should feel about these things, but this may not accord with the whirlwind of our actual feelings. My argument is that if we cannot be honest with ourselves and take care of what are often infantile responses in ourselves, we are in danger of acting out our feelings and not helping our patients.

I am describing an environment that challenges at many levels the equilibrium of the people working in it. We all have ambivalent feelings about mothers and babies. The sight of well mothers and well babies preoccupied with each other, getting to know and fall in love with each other, stirs everyone, although we may sceptically defend ourselves against this. One may identify with the mother and long for a baby of one's own; one may have to cope with fears that one will never have a baby or with the knowledge that one cannot, or with the memory of a lost baby; one may have to face the fact that that time of one's life is over, which entails a more immediate recognition of one's own mortality. Or one may identify with the baby and have to face the longing to be loved and looked after again in that special way, or the mourning that that did not happen, if that was not your experience. Of course, there are other characters in this scenario—the father, the siblings, the grandparents. One may feel left out, as these characters often do, or struggling to have a part, to be helpful and to bear not having a central role. As I have argued in chapter 6, the sight of a mother and baby is a very powerful one, which moves us in all kinds of ways and sometimes activates our spite.

In the NICU we have another line of defence: one would not choose to be one of these mothers or babies. So staff on the unit have to cope with a very complex and shifting emotional situation, where they are surrounded by babies and all that this means, and also by the wish not to have a baby like this. Doctors and nurses sometimes avoid being involved with the babies; on the other hand, I see them holding them, I hear of doctors cuddling babies in the middle of the night, and, once in a staff support meeting, one nurse talked about how wonderfully soft a particular baby was and was met with laughter and teasing about how much she cuddled it and wry comments about how the rota would have to be changed to put an end to this. It seems that we are envious even of these mothers and babies, though we can easily tell ourselves that we are not. When we deal with well babies, we can reassure ourselves that our envy has not damaged them, even that we may have been able to be helpful. On the unit, when there is a good outcome, staff can feel that they have been of use. When a baby dies or, I think, worse still, is in terrible pain and does not die, then everyone's sense of goodness is under attack. This is when rows flare up.

My view is that if it can be acknowledged that there are these complicated aspects to work on a NICU, if these feelings are articulated, staff can deal with them more easily, sometimes even with humour. Where they are unacknowledged, staff are struggling with intolerable feelings and are often unaware of what they are up against.

I want to consider two vignettes of unit life with these ideas in mind.

* * *

My first story is about a staff support meeting at which three nurses, whom I shall call "Annabel", "Bonny", and "Caroline", were present. Dr Gibbons (the child psychiatrist) and myself were there to convene the meeting. As people assembled, there was talk of being on strike, laughter, and the usual awkwardness and ambivalence about coming to this meeting. There was some talk about this being like a trade union meeting. There was some discussion about whether we had talked about baby "Mandy". Dr Gibbons and I said that she had been talked about last week, when none of them were here, and the week before, when Nurse Annabel was present. They decided they would talk about her. And Nurse Bonny, who said that it was so very sad, took on the task of reminding Dr Gibbons about this baby. This was a baby whose mother had had cancer, and she had become seriously ill while she was carrying the baby. It seemed that she had hung on to life as long as she could, to give her baby life. The baby was born prematurely, and soon afterwards the mother died. The father was looking after the baby day by day on the unit, with infinite care and love, and was soon to be joined by his mother, who came from another country.

Nurse Annabel said that there were so many different stories. Had the mother known that she had cancer when she became pregnant? Nurse Bonny said that the cancer had got a lot worse when she was pregnant. Nurse Annabel remarked that it was the worst thing that could happen to a mother—to have to leave her baby. There was general talk about how father was doing very well, and that he seemed rather motherly. I said that perhaps it helped him with his loss of his wife to be like her, to take on her role. Then there was some talk about whether she had known before she died that she had had the baby. Someone said that she had held it; but Nurse Annabel said that there were no photographs, that father would not allow them.

This was a very painful case, and the nurses had talked quite a lot before the baby came to the unit about how they would cope, whether the mother was alive or dead. There seemed to be a lot of admiration for this mother, who had struggled to stay alive to give her baby life, and of her labour, which took place as she was dying. There was also admiration for the father, who was quiet and rather dignified and not obviously asking for help. Some remarks suggested that there was a wish to find someone to blame for this painful experience—mother for getting pregnant when she had cancer, father for not allowing photographs—but none of this really took off, and there was an atmosphere of sadness in the room.

Then Nurse Annabel said, rolling her eyes, that she had been to a planning meeting with the social workers about arrangements for baby "Harriet" after he was discharged from the unit. She then told Dr Gibbons about this case. The mother, Miss "White", was young and had a history of abuse. The baby was premature. The mother was a prostitute, and the father, an older man, was her pimp. Nurse Annabel said that he wanted her back at work, that he lived with another woman who was his wife, and that there was some idea that he wanted the baby to be brought up by her. Miss White's sister, who was 15, was pregnant by the same man. I pointed out that he used Miss White's earnings to support his family. Nurse Annabel said with some anger that when they had told mother that the wife had visited the unit, Miss White had said what a nice woman she was. Then there was some talk about what they would like to do to this man. There was quite a lot of laughter, and handcuffing was suggested, more laughter as Nurse Bonny said no, castration. They wondered how he could get away with it. And they were angry that they had to be civil to him. Then there was a discussion about what hope there could be for this baby. I said that it all seemed quite exciting, a bit like a television series— not as painful as the case of the other baby we had been talking about. Dr Gibbons agreed that it seemed easier to talk about this baby; we could be moralistic, we knew what we thought, we could even be funny, we could feel that we were not like these people. With baby Mandy, on the other hand, there was no one to blame, and so we were left with the pain.

It seemed that the discussion of baby Mandy was felt to be too painful, and it was with a sense of relief that the group had turned to baby Harriet. They recounted all the lurid details of the story, and I joined in. It had the atmosphere of "and then do you know what happened . . .". Perhaps we were all turning to Dr Gibbons to tell him this terrible story with the idea that he should sort it out and see that justice was done. The father was certainly an ideal candidate for hatred. Perhaps the thoughts about what baby Mandy's mother had gone through felt too much. Nurse Annabel, herself a mother, identified very strongly with the pain of this mother having to leave her baby. And then all accounts of the mother had been of her dignity and courage. This did not seem a very needy couple where one could feel reassured by their need for one's support. The parents had been very close and self-con-tained. Perhaps there was only space for admiration, and it was hard to go on giving that.

At this point Nurse Caroline suddenly began talking about baby "Kenneth". The mother, she said, had attacked her verbally— nothing she did was right. She would wash the baby's face but not his neck, and so on. I asked Nurse Annabel whether there had been any more complaints from baby Kenneth's mother. In a rather subdued way Dr Gibbons was told that this was a prema-ture baby where a nursing accident had probably occurred, and the mother was threatening to complain officially. None of these particular nurses was involved in this incident. Nurse Caroline interrupted and said that she wanted to finish: that the mother had washed the baby and had not dried him properly and had put oil on the top, that it made her feel awful to watch this. I said that this mother had always complained, but more so since the accident. Nurse Caroline said that it was awful to be treated like this by mothers when you were doing your best for their babies. I said that the mothers were angry, they wished that they had lovely, healthy full-term babies to take home, they hated being here; that they directed this hatred at the nurses. Dr Gibbons said that the nurses did not just have to take it. He wondered what they could say to the mothers—something like: "I know that I am doing it right, why do you think that I am not?" Or talk to her about its not being fair. The nurses all thought about this.

I said that it often seemed as if I was saying that they had to accept all of this bad temper. At a previous meeting, Nurse Annabel had said that they did not want to hear any more excuses from me. She grinned and mentioned Ms "Davis", another mother on the NICU. Nurse Bonny exclaimed: "It was so awful, she was so rude!" Nurse Caroline said that she went into the parents' room to take the heater for baby Kenneth, and Ms Davis said, "Oh, you're taking my heater now." And Nurse Caroline said that she thought it had NICU written on it. Dr Gibbons talked about the mothers abusing the staff—how to hand it back, or maybe the nurses just wanted to unload it on us the way the mothers did on them. I said that I was not sure about "abuse". I thought that some of the mothers were so deprived that they had no experience of some- where to put their anger. Ms Davis had said that she could not understand the unit—you were rude, and people told you off, but they were friendly the next day. But this was an experience most people had when they were children in their families. I wondered whether there was an issue between her and the nurse about whose home the unit is. Dr Gibbons said: "So you mean that they are using the nurses a bit as mothers?" And I said, yes but that that was hard on the nurses. They have the babies as patients and the mothers as well. Then Dr Gibbons said that we were saying rather different things, that he was trying to be supportive, stressing how hard it was to take all of this and how the nurses might talk to the mothers. Whereas I was saying that the mothers sometimes needed to put their anger somewhere and have it understood. He said that if we can just be angry with the parents, it's easier for us; if we start to understand them, it becomes more painful for us—we might have to understand baby Harriet's mother and even, un- thinkably, her man.

The meeting finished with some more jollity, about breaking the strike, locking themselves up in the room, not going back to the nursery to work, and it was mentioned that they had not had any lunch.

It is interesting to note that when Dr Gibbons had talked about our wish to blame the parents because, when we could not, these situations were so painful, Nurse Caroline had begun to talk about a case where she was being blamed by the mother. So the nurses escaped from having to face how they blamed the mothers and then became the victims of the mothers' intolerable criticism and then rudeness. Dr Gibbons and I thought differently about this. He was more protective of the nurses, helping them to deal with their masochism and to learn how to be more straightforward in handing back some of this in a reasonable way to the mothers. I felt that the mothers are often coping with intolerable circumstances and that the nurses, by understanding this, can help them. It raises the interesting question of when it is helpful to hold someone's anger, to stifle one's own response, and when it is necessary to draw a boundary. The thought that one might be asked to understand any person raised the awful idea that even this pimp might be within human boundaries. The idea was greeted with some laughter, but perhaps the nurses did feel invaded and like locking themselves up in the room. They reminded us that they had not had lunch. This is a recurrent theme in staff support meetings, where the staff think of themselves as being very hardy, able to exist on very little, with very few demands, as Dr Gibbons has pointed out, enduring their lot like soldiers in an army. Dr Gibbons and I, on the contrary, are thought of as being soft and perhaps coming up with soft ideas. The staff respond with ambivalence about these. The meeting moved from something very painful to an abusive story and then to circumstances where the nurses were the ones who were feeling badly treated.

* * *

My second story is of a baby who was born at 28 weeks of gestation and weighed 500 grams at birth, with severe growth retardation. Baby "Joseph" was ventilated with very high levels of oxygen and came to have very damaged lungs. He was thought to be in great danger from the beginning. The parents were West Indian. They had a 19-year-old daughter; they had had no children since. Mother's parents had gone back to the West Indies the previous year, and mother had become pregnant. Mother, a very actively religious woman, found it hard to use time with me for her own needs. She would either enquire how I was or reiterate her own faith. However, she gradually told me about her own childhood, about how much she missed her parents, about how very ill she had been throughout this pregnancy, about how worried she was by her daughter's feelings about the baby, and about how the only person she was quarrelling with was her husband.

During the first few weeks of baby Joseph's life, most medical and nursing staff thought that he would die, that his prognosis was so poor and that he was in sufficient discomfort to consider just maintaining care and not striving to keep him alive. The parents, however, wanted everything possible done. They invited friends to the unit and had a prayer meeting, and this was repeated. By the time baby Joseph was 6 weeks old, Dr Kennedy, the consultant paediatrician, said that he could not survive, that he was in pain, and that it was her advice that treatment should just be to keep him as comfortable as possible. She was obviously upset at having to keep this baby alive, and she told the parents that in her view it was cruel to go on with treatment, and that it could be hard for the nurses to take care of him. The parents said that they understood what she was saying but that they wanted to continue. Mother was very upset and began to ring in the night to ask the nurses if it was hard for them. They began to side with her and to say no, of course not, and to say among themselves that the doctor was unkind to have said such a thing. Because several times this baby had not died when it was thought that he would and because of mother's very manifest religious belief, there grew up a feeling that baby Joseph might survive. But his stomach was very badly distended and full of pus. All of this raised a lot of anger in the unit.

One day I came into the unit to be confronted by a group of nurses who said that they wanted a meeting. I pointed out that there was to be a meeting on both the following day and the day after. No, they said, it had to be now. So we met: Dr Kennedy, the registrar, two SHOs, a manager, and three nurses—Caroline, Ann, and Sally. I asked Nurse Caroline, who had asked for the meeting, to say something about what the nurses were feeling. She said that they felt that mother had been pushed into a corner and that she was very upset. Dr Kennedy told how she had talked to mother, trying, on the one hand, to take some of the responsibility away from her by saying that it was not the parents' decision, that it was her advice to withdraw treatment but that on the other it would not be done without their agreement—nothing would be done behind their backs or without their agreement. I said that I thought it was true that mother was in a corner, that she had been shielded by her religious beliefs from thinking that baby Joseph would die, and now she was confronted by the idea that it might be cruel to keep him alive; that this was a difficult place to be in, but it was where she was. It was no wonder that she was angry and upset, and that the staff were responding to that and then perhaps taking their anger out on Dr Kennedy. After all, it was easier to be angry than to be sad.

Dr Kennedy then talked about the baby's terrible medical condition—that it was a wonder that he could still be alive. His stomach was full of thick green pus: there was a question about why the antibiotics had not worked. The nurses said that they were angry because the treatment plan was unclear. They asked why, if things were this bad, they were not just giving palliative care; why should he have to put up with his eyes being tested, and why were they drawing off the pus. Dr Kennedy said that she did not know why his eyes had been tested, but that they were drawing pus from an abscess just under the skin, which she thought was probably draining into the pus in the stomach, and she was doing this because she was afraid that it might burst, afraid that his whole stomach might burst open. I said that to a non-medical person this sounded dreadful. Dr Kennedy said that it was, that his stomach might burst open, with pus and guts flying everywhere. Nurse Caroline agreed that his skin would break down. An SHO said that she had spoken to mother, had told her to cry, to scream if she wanted, that they were sisters, that she should let it out, that it was not good to keep it in. She thought that she was nearer to agreeing to withdraw treatment.

I thought that this doctor was expressing the feelings of the group—that there was a real feeling of horror at the breakdown of this baby's body, some panic about how to manage it, and some idea that these were intolerable thoughts that had to be evacuated. The manager said that she was worried about the effect on the other parents: they heard and they saw, and shouldn't baby Joseph be in a side-room? This brought a storm from the nurses, who said, "What? Left alone to die? Oh, no!" It was then pointed out that there might very well be problems arising about infection. The nurses said that then they would be moving him for that reason, and that would be different, but that he should not be isolated. Dr Kennedy then said that she had spoken to mother—what was the point of speaking again? I said that mother and father had to digest all of this. The mother would probably fluctuate, her states of mind would change, and that at times she would hate those who gave her bad news. It was agreed that Dr Kennedy and I would meet the parents once a week.

All of these issues continued to be discussed on the unit: thoughts about the pain that baby Joseph was going through, night-mare thoughts about his skin splitting or coming off, thoughts about the parents and what was going on in their minds, the wish that he had died three weeks before and saved himself and every-one else from this kind of torture. With this latter thought came thoughts about the investment made in the babies: did this count as a life, was it something to be valued for itself, was there any way of feeling all right about any of this?

It was nearly a month after this meeting that baby Joseph died, quite quickly, one night. No one seemed surprised except Dr Kennedy, who kept on puzzling about why he had died then. The nurses felt surprised and rather persecuted by her enquiry—they felt that she had, after all, been saying for weeks that he could not stay alive. I reflected on my own states of mind throughout all of this. I had believed Dr Kennedy when she said that baby Joseph could not survive, but I was aware, every now and then, at the edge of my mind, of a feeling of hope: perhaps all this talk about how he always came through was right, maybe he would make it. I would eradicate these thoughts as irrational, magical, something to be repressed and ashamed of. But in this reflective state I thought that I had to face them and to consider whether it was only possible to continue if there was a glimmer of hope, however small. I then wondered about Dr Kennedy's state of mind. I had assumed that her mind was clearly in one state—a sort of medical, scientific state, quite unlike the mess of my thoughts. I then won-dered whether she, too, had harboured some hope for baby Joseph quite against the rest of her mind, and that his death was a disappointment and a blow to her. I felt that I had let her down in not keeping her vulnerability in mind.

* * *

This story illustrates the states of mind that staff get into in the face of such painful experiences and how these can sometimes be tolerated but how they are often resisted in a variety of ways. A common defence is to become angry, to blame someone and then to hate them—this eradicates the pain. Another is to withdraw into a cool analytic state, to be critical of the emotional mess everyone else is getting into and to take refuge in some cut-and-dried solution that denies the complexity of the situation. A third is to get on with your work—to put your head down and to refuse to engage. A fourth is to get into a rubbery, indifferent, or cruel state of mind where these things do not matter—they simply have no meaning. My job is to help people to recognize these states of mind in themselves and so to help them not to be run by them; to recognize them and to be interested in them in that they not only say something about the people themselves but also about the situation they are facing. So instead of being an inconvenience or a persecution, one's feelings can become important tools for work. The articulation of these states on the unit, in meetings, and in a book like this is meant to be a support to staff. People are often afraid that they will be hopelessly overwhelmed by feelings, whereas experience seems to show us that they are more troublesome when unattended to—that once they are owned, they seem to become more human and manageable.

In this chapter I have concentrated on the impact on staff of the babies and their parents; I have not looked outwards in the web to the effect of government policy on the working conditions of all staff, to the bad working conditions, the overwork, the threats of merger and redundancy. These undoubtedly add to the stress suffered by the staff.

* * *

The day I began this chapter, I had an appointment to see a mother whose baby had died some 3½ weeks before. For several months,

Mrs "Brown" had constantly visited her baby on the unit. At first the baby had done very well, but then he had deteriorated. She was a mother whom I liked very much. She told me much about her own life, and I felt that she liked to talk to me and that I could be useful to her. Her baby had got worse and had been taken to Great Ormond Street Hospital. One Tuesday I went to visit the mother and baby there. It was hard to talk to her—her friend was there, and the nurses seemed very manic. They insisted on getting the baby out of the ventilator, although the mother was clearly terrified, and then they took lots of photos. We had just got talking, and then the camera was again intruded for another round of photos. However, she did find time to talk, and I was glad to have seen her.

The following day the baby died. I spoke to the mother on the telephone about how it had all been. I was going on holiday and would miss the funeral, and we arranged to meet as soon as I got back. She did not turn up to our meeting. She left a message at my home and on the unit to say that she could not make it. That night I had a dream:[1]

I was seeing this mother with another woman, who was also on the unit, in a room like the unit coffee-room but larger. We were talking, and someone burst in. They left when I pointed out that I was using the room . We began again. Then a young, confident woman marched in, followed by a horde of students. I remonstrated with her, but she was immovable. I hissed at her that this woman's baby had died. She did not bat an eyelid. I began to attack her physically, pulling her hair, pushing her, and so on. The thought bubbled around in my mind that this was not very professional, and that I would pay for it later. I restrained myself and fell into convulsive weeping. I wondered how I could face this mother after making such a fuss about this, compared to what she had gone through. I also thought that I would not be able to go out on to the unit with red eyes.

As I awoke, I thought that this grief must really be about the baby dying. Well, perhaps it was about the baby dying, and also about what this mother, my patient, had gone through. Perhaps this mother had not turned up to our meeting because I had been away on holiday, I had not been there to comfort her in the loss of her baby—full of importance, like the young woman in the dream, who interrupted the intimate time between me and the mother. But there may be another way of looking at this dream. This young woman, obviously of childbearing age, had pushed her way into my room with all of her eager babies (her students). There was no acknowledgement of my work, that it might take skill, or need privacy, or be of any value—my baby was deemed of no significance. I had felt rejected by the mother, who had not turned up that afternoon. Was I of no use, empty, whereas those around me were full of life and riches? . . . presumably very much the feeling of this mother as well? I think that that was what my fury was about: not only had my patient's baby died, but my work, my baby, seemed to be of no value, and I was redundant, past it, whereas others were effortlessly productive (my competitor in the dream had a "horde" of students). I think our work is closely linked to our sense of fertility—hence, in part, our rage and grief when a baby dies, or is in terrible pain, and we can do nothing.

Note

1. I am grateful to Wilhelmina Kraemer-Zurné for discussion of this dream. Her view was that I had not thought sufficiently about the impact of my holiday on this woman because of the weight of being so important to somebody in this position and that I preferred the view of myself as old and unfruitful, in identification with how this woman was feeling.

CHAPTER NINE

Doctors, midwives, and prison officers

> As it is, the quickest of us walk about well wadded with
> stupidity.
>
> George Eliot, *Middlemarch*

D r Gibbons, the child psychiatrist, and I were convinced of the importance of staff support in hospitals. We shared the view of the web of relationships described in chapter 8, and in this chapter I have written about various other pieces of work that sprang from our neonatal staff support work.

* * *

We became aware of the need of the consultant paediatricians for a support meeting of their own. We began meeting with three of the four consultants once a month; the fourth was invited but refused to attend. The content of these meetings varied considerably, from a recounting of painful cases, discussion of NHS politics, and plans and issues in the paediatric department. Over the years, this group has grown larger with the appointment of more consultant paediatricians. Perhaps the group has become less cosy; there has been more space for misunderstanding and disagreement. There are certainly generational tensions, with some tussle for floor-space between the older consultants and the younger ones. We are always struck by how hard-working and thoughtful this group is and how difficult it is for the members to let each other speak. There is definitely an atmosphere of there not being enough attention to go around.

* * *

A second and less successful offshoot of our neonatal work has been staff support with the midwives. Quite naturally, the NICU and the midwives have patients in common. Midwives sometimes attended the neonatal staff support meeting when there had been a difficult birth with neonatal involvement. This led to a request from the midwives for their own support meetings. With some difficulty we found a midday time when the midwives were having an hour and a quarter hand-over; this meant that some midwives could be spared to come to the meeting.

The first two meetings were packed. They were held on the labour ward. At the first meeting a black midwife began by asking why the midwives should put up with so much verbal abuse. She was full of life and passion, and she apologised again and again for speaking. She told us about how a patient had sworn at her on the telephone that morning. As she filled in the story, there were murmurs of recognition and agreement from other midwives. She went on to say that it was hard being a midwife in the community too—that there was a lot of violence and "racist stuff". She said that sometimes people did not want a black midwife to examine their baby. Another said that patients became more abusive once the baby was born. Yet another said that she put it down to inflation—they were given fewer flowers and chocolates these days. There was general agreement that they were the recipients of less gratitude.

As the nurses spoke, there was a constant stream of people coming and going in and out of the room, and a very squeaky door, which people seemed almost deliberately to open and close. Perhaps we were meant to experience working in very difficult circumstances.

The subject continued to be that of violence. The midwives asked what the point was in talking about how awful their work was. Dr Gibbons, who was the only man in the room, said that perhaps they felt that they wanted something done, some protection given. They asked more about who we were and about the neonatal unit meetings. Someone said that they needed somewhere to talk. The midwife who had spoken first described how, when patients were rude and abusive, you felt like . . . and she made a gesture of strangling. I said that it seemed that they were overwhelmed by feelings of violence, both from outside and from inside, and that I thought that that must be very hard to cope with. Several nurses murmured assent and went on to talk about their murderous feelings towards patients. Then one midwife said that all of this affected how you behaved at home—it made you sharper with your own children—and she made a gesture of swatting the air with a rolled-up piece of paper. I was struck by two midwives using gestures to express their feelings and thought that perhaps they were afraid of articulating them, as if they would turn out to be too horrible for words.

One midwife wanted more security on the door to the postnatal wards. Another talked about the chaos on these wards. She said that there were too many visitors, there was too much noise, that the midwives felt that they had no authority, and that it was a dangerous situation, where baby-snatching could take place. Others said that the mothers got tired and then did not want to look after their babies.

There was a wish that the old nurses' uniforms could be brought back. They felt that they would get dignity and authority from these—that they could not be distinguished from the domestics in their present uniforms. There was nostalgia for the traditional frilly caps, and two older midwives described how they had theirs carefully packed away at home. I asked who the ward belonged to. I had thought that it was supposed to be ruled by a hierarchy of nurses; it seemed, according to the midwives, as if the parents acted like unruly adolescents, partying and refusing to obey the rules, and that they did not know how to assert their authority. There was a general grumbling response to this. The nurse manager present launched into an impassioned speech, saying that the team system did not work, that there was no one clearly in charge, that the best nurses went into the community, and that the hospital was left with agency nurses. She said that she was often frantic and knew the service was unsafe. Another nurse manager reported that she had been completely burnt out during the previous winter.

We were struck by the sense of hopelessness and by the absence of any idea of being able to recuperate themselves or improve their working conditions. When Dr Gibbons asked how they were going to proceed, the nurses became quite directionless. We suggested to them that we might meet for staff support, that we felt that they were flooded with feelings of rage and impotence and were often terrified at work and that there was a clear absence of leadership or authority. When we mentioned the experience of some parents having a new baby and the importance and fears involved in this, it was ignored—as if the midwives' needs were so unattended to that they could not manage to think imaginatively about the patients.

At the second meeting we heard how frightening it was to be a community midwife. They described how dangerous it was to go out at night to supervise home deliveries, that it would often be difficult to find the right address, and they would be afraid of assault. They said, ruefully, that even the police worked in pairs, whereas they had to go out on their own. We were again struck by their desperate working conditions.

A manager came to the third meeting and was criticized for the conditions of work. The midwives showed their anger. Soon after this, the hand-over time was cut to a quarter of an hour, and there was no longer time for our meetings. Whether or not this was done to sabotage the meeting, we never knew; I doubt that it was consciously done for this reason. In any case, the cutting of hand-over time to a quarter of an hour was symptomatic of what the midwives were complaining of. It is impossible to give a thoughtful hand-over in a quarter of an hour. There can be no interest shown in individual mothers, babies, and families, only the bare minimum can be done, and work becomes less satisfying and interesting for the midwives.

Our attempts to help this group failed. We heard later that the meetings had been appreciated. We certainly believed that the midwives needed this kind of support. Apart from the difficulties of their working conditions, they often had to deal with frightening and tragic situations. It is their job to support mothers and families, and they get very little help with their responses to all of this.

* * *

Accident and Emergency was another area that we ventured into. Again this was because of the overlap with the NICU and paediatrics. We have not had regular meetings but have convened special ones when traumatic incidents with babies or children occurred in Accident and Emergency. We have had several meetings where a child has been brought in dead or has died in hospital. We are grateful to the energy and commitment of the consultant paediatricians, who have set up these meetings because of their belief that staff need to talk after a death. They have been imaginative in their awareness of the web of relationships in the hospital: so sometimes GPs have been invited, as well as local social workers, health visitors, ambulance staff, and the medical staff involved at the hospital. They have become adept at remembering if there were locum staff involved who should be invited back to the meeting or students who have since finished their placement. Usually in these meetings the story of the incident gets told with staff taking it in turns to fill in the details. Sometimes the telling of this story reminds individuals of events that have occurred perhaps years earlier, about which they have never talked and which they have carried painfully ever since. These meetings seem worthwhile to us, and we are aware that we are dependent on the commitment of senior doctors to make them happen.

* * *

Outside the hospital, we have arranged some staff support meetings at the local women's prison. This involvement springs from the neonatal work, because the unit serves the prison. The incidence of prematurity in babies of prison inmates is higher than that in the general population, and so there is often a baby in the NICU whose mother is in the prison. Many of these mothers gain a place in the Mother and Baby Unit in the prison. It was to this unit that we sought to gain entrance.

Our reception by the prison and, more specifically, by the Mother and Baby Unit was mixed. We were invited to come, but usually our appointment was forgotten. We would have to wait at the main entrance while phone-calls were made and our identity checked. We both noticed that Dr Gibbons, a man and a doctor, was addressed, while I was often treated as invisible. We would be allowed through the double gates and told to wait. Once, while we were waiting in this area to leave, the gates were frozen because someone was missing, which meant that nobody was allowed in or out of the prison. We were told by someone who was also waiting to leave that the last time this had happened, it was many hours before the gates were unfrozen and he was let out. Thoughts about our outside commitments became dominant in our minds. Luckily for us, the gates were unfrozen quite soon, but we were forcibly reminded of the custodial reality of this institution.

We would usually be collected after some time from this area and taken to the Mother and Baby Unit. This journey was along wide corridors, through many heavily locked doors, and up barred lifts. We always seemed to go by a different route, and it was hard to have any sense of direction. It was with relief that we left this bleak, menacing environment and arrived at the Mother and Baby Unit, with its familiar baby paraphernalia. This unit can take thirteen mothers and babies at a time.

Over the years that we visited the prison unit, we were struck by the high turnover of staff, particularly the governors of that unit. These governors were invariably welcoming, they had an enormous amount to say themselves, they had a very moving concern for the women prisoners and consideration for their staff, and they stayed in the post for quite short periods of time. They seemed very keen for their staff to have support and usually said that they would attend the next meeting—but at the next meeting it was almost always forgotten, although it would have been "put down in the book".

Every time we attended, some kind of meeting would take place, officers would be found who could attend, and the meetings were always fascinating. Over the years, there were one or two prison officers whom we saw regularly. The meetings would be attended by prison officers, nursery nurses, and sometimes the unit governor.

The discussion would often centre around a particular mother. This might be someone by whom they felt provoked, or it might be someone who they felt worried about. A young woman might have been on the unit who had been in an abusive relationship outside. The officers would have talked to her and may have felt that she had made progress in extricating herself from this. At one meeting such a story was recounted, and we were told that the woman had just been released. The anxiety about how she was coping was palpable. It was as if this young woman had left home, and her parents were worrying about how she was managing in the cruel outside world. She had, as was usually the case, a history of deprivation, and it sounded as if this might have been the first bit of mothering that she had had.

We noticed that the prison officers' work was both custodial and therapeutic and that they had conflicting feelings. Some officers coming from other parts of the prison hated working on the Mother and Baby Unit. They felt that it was "soft", that the function of prison as punishment was lost. One officer said that an important part of their work was to say no. Other officers who always worked on the unit liked the therapeutic and "rescuing" aspect of it and did not like working in other parts of the prison.

Sometimes the officers talked about dealing with women who had harmed themselves—about the horrible details of this. They also talked about attacks on themselves. One woman officer started to tell us in a very matter-of-fact way about being beaten up by a prisoner on another block; she said that this had not affected her. But as the story unravelled, we heard that she had suffered from severe weight loss, insomnia, and bouts of anxiety and depression. We were aware of her trauma in a way that she did not seem able to be, the culture of denial was so strong.

As the officers talked to us of their own lives, we realized that they were often very deprived people themselves. One officer told us that they could easily have gone astray themselves, but that they had not. This affected their view of their work with the prisoners, some wanting to help them, some to punish them. Some officers felt that it was not fair that the prisoners got looked after more than the officers did.

Officers explored their thoughts about babies being in prison: after all, they had not done anything wrong. They wondered whether it was better for them to be fostered or adopted or to be with their mothers. They often asked us for a judgement on this. In this prison babies were allowed to stay with their mothers until they were 9 months old; then they had to go either to the family outside or for fostering. Another possibility was for the mother to get a transfer to another women's prison in the north of England, where babies could stay until they were 18 months old. Officers wondered if this just put off the terrible moment of separation for women who had long sentences, and if it would be better for these babies never to have known their mothers. We heard of the months of uncertainty a mother would have to endure to see if her application for transfer would be accepted. At this time I was supervising someone who was writing a thesis on the prison Mother and Baby Unit and observing the babies. It seemed very clear that the mothers' despair and uncertainty wore away at the quality of the attachment between the mother and baby. It was very painful to hear the observations of one baby, who had had very good contact with his mother, gradually becoming depressed in the face of her withdrawal as the date of separation drew near.

Nursery nurses had been hired by the unit with the idea that the babies needed thinking about. In fact when this was being planned, we were asked for our comments and approval. This appointment proved complicated. Actually, many of the officers liked playing with the babies and seemed to resent the nursery nurses. Also, some officers felt that the mothers treated the nursery like a crèche rather than taking responsibility for the babies themselves. This became part of a general complaint: that the women did not cook for their babies or shop for them—although of course they were not allowed to—and that they complained if they were asked to wash the floor. So the officers sometimes thought of them as spoiled—as if the unit were a hotel! The mothers have their own very small rooms, where they sleep with their babies. During the day they are allowed to mix with the other mothers and babies, but at night, from 8 p.m. until 7:45 a.m., they are confined to their rooms. Many women find this a frightening and claustrophobic experience.

Some officers also worked in the block where pregnant women were kept, and some in a block they called "Medicals", where mentally ill prisoners were kept. These officers had terrible tales of cutting down women who had hanged themselves, and of the frightening levels of violence they experienced. The women on "Medicals" might be "banged up" for 23 hours of the day if staffing levels were very low. A macabre kind of humour was used by the officers to ward off feeling in the telling of these incidents. Sometimes it seemed that we were meant to have all the feeling, and the meetings often left us feeling horrified.

Our meetings usually ended with a request for more meetings and plans about whom to invite to attend and how to regularize our contact. But when we would attend for the next meeting, we would almost invariably be met by different people. We came to think that life and thinking were carried out on very much a day-to-day basis, and that it was almost impossible for the thread of attachment to survive. Hopelessness and terror were so prevalent that it became hard to think or even to remember plans and decisions that had been made.

Even our own attachment to the prison was fragile. A younger colleague asked to join us for one visit and took on working with Medicals after a particularly ghastly description of this block. Our contact with the unit petered out. We were no doubt relieved that someone young and enthusiastic would take over. But there was something about the way we felt so invisible, so unnecessary, so totally replaceable, in a way that mirrored the ethos of the institution. I think that we wanted to be rid of our contact in much the same way that society wants to be rid of these women. It has been pointed out how unnecessary custodial sentences are for many of the women in prison. In fact, between 1993 and 1998, the number of women prisoners increased by 100%. Many women have been given long sentences for acting as "mules"—bringing in drugs for dealers who will probably not be caught and whose profit from the woman's risk is much greater than the woman's would ever be. Some are in prison for shoplifting or burglary, but very few for violent crimes. So there is a question to be answered about why we lock so many women up. It may be argued that some women will be deterred from crime because of the fear of being locked up, and so custodial sentences are in order. But the brutalization of those who are locked up and the fragmentation of their families' lives should make us more alarmed by this trend.

The prison itself has been the subject of much adverse criticism, both because of its filthy conditions and because of overcrowding. Many of the women are unconvicted, held on remand until their trial date. It is said that the nights can be frightening times, with the women screaming, banging on windows, and sometimes setting fire to bedding. Officers report that because of their under-staffing, they often feel unsafe. A few of the pregnant women are still handcuffed to a warder on the way to the hospital and during labour. The publicity around a woman who was kept in shackles during labour at our hospital in 1996 may have made this practice less common. This woman was shackled to two strangers, one of them a man. During that same year, another woman prisoner was shackled during the funeral of her 10-day-old baby. Both of these events brought a storm of protest from doctors and nurses and particularly from the Royal College of Midwives. Caroline Flint, the president of the Royal College of Midwives, had a clear perspective; she was reported in *The Guardian* (11 January 1996) as saying: "In a civilized country, women who have children or are pregnant should not be in prison unless they are absolutely a danger to themselves or society."

It does seem that such humiliating practices are further examples of our cruelty to mothers and of how we attack their relationships with their babies. In this case, the cruelty seems to have become embedded in our institutional practices. Those looking after offending women need help to think about their task and support in doing their job in a constructive way. There is no official—or unofficial—recognition of the therapeutic support that some officers are giving the mothers. The work that we did was very infrequent and not properly established within the institution. It was clear that there was a great appetite for discussion—that officers needed to have a forum to discuss their differing ideas of their job, their feelings about individual women, and their worries about particular babies and their difficulties in losing them when they left the unit because they had become so attached to them. If an opportunity is not given, officers come to think of attachment as something to be avoided, and then humanity cannot flourish. Properly thought about, a Mother and Baby Unit such as this could be an extraordinary opportunity for the mothers, the babies, and probably also for the officers. As it is, mothers who are imprisoned often lose their children, their homes, and their jobs, and the cycle of disaster is perpetuated.

CHAPTER TEN

Addiction

... and feel by turns the bitter change
Of fierce extremes, extremes by change more fierce,
From beds of raging fire to starve in ice
Their soft ethereal warmth, and there to pine
Immovable, infixed, and frozen round,
Periods of time, thence hurried back to fire,

Milton, *Paradise Lost*, 2.11.598

One autumn the atmosphere in the cool nursery of the NICU was bad. There were two babies withdrawing from heroin, along with several other difficult babies. But it was these two babies who created an atmosphere of irritability. One, "Jilly", was on methadone. At the beginning of October she was 3 weeks old, her mother was sick with AIDS, and her father was unaware of her illness or of her drug problem; because the parents were not married, the staff were bound by confidentiality on these issues and so could not inform the father. The other baby, "Debbie", was also on methadone. She was 3 weeks old, she was stiff, and there were worries about her long-term neurological state. Her parents were both drug-users and seemed to consume a

173

lot of alcohol. So there were social work worries about whether these babies should go home with their mothers.

* * *

At this time I was quite often aware of how irritable the nurses were in the cool nursery, how much at the end of their tether, how open they were in their dislike, particularly of Jilly, who screamed almost all the time that she was awake. I decided to spend more time in the cool nursery and to record my observations of Jilly.

I had often heard Jilly's awful, piercing scream, but when I came into the Nursery when she was 4 weeks old, she was quiet. I was told that she was now on methadone only once a day, and that she had had a very bad night. Jilly was in her pram on her tummy, face to her right, mouth and nose into the ruffled sheeting. It was very unusual for a baby to be in a pram, and this was an indication of how difficult the nurses were finding her. She was there so that she could be pushed around in an attempt to calm her.

She was making little mouth movements, her eyelids fluttered, and her eyes moved under her lids. Overall she looked so still that I was amazed at the constant movement of her eyes and mouth. These little movements went on for some time, and then she nestled into the sheet with her head, as if she were burrowing, struggling a bit, and rubbing her nose. Then she rubbed her mouth and nose from side to side; the sheet was very ruckled up, and her face was into it. There was a lot of noise going on around her, but she did not respond to it at all. Debbie next to her was screaming, but Jilly did not seem to notice. The nurses began to be worried about whether to feed her, because it was now five and a half hours since her last feed. One nurse picked her up, and she immediately started crying.

She put her down and got the feed ready. Jilly was crying and rubbing her eyes. Jilly took the offered bottle and fixed her gaze on the two light panels on the ceiling. The nurse complained that she had not wanted to wake her up, but it was unit policy, but that it was silly, because the policy was for premature babies, and Jilly was not premature. Jilly took the bottle without any interest; her hands, white with pressure, were placed on each other on her chest. The nurse commented that she was not really taking anything and took the bottle away to show me. The nurse continued complaining that she had had such a good feed at nine o'clock and that now she wanted to sleep, but that it was policy, she had to do it. At this moment Debbie's father left the nursery, flicking on the radio as he went out of the door, so that we were all subjected to the noise.

I thought that Jilly had found some peace from her internal torment and that she was burrowing into the mattress trying to get even further from her tormentors. She had no interest in being fed, and the nurse knew this but could not take responsibility for having her own thoughts, so she mindlessly followed Policy, which became the tyrant with power over both of them. Jilly gazed at the light panels—an institutional baby, who finds the fixed physical surroundings more comforting than the multiplicity of nurses who look after her. I felt a wave of rage sweep over me as all the disturbance seemed to be epitomized by Debbie's father's action as he left the nursery.

I came into the Nursery the next day, and it was quiet, but Nurse Nancy said that I should have heard both babies screaming just before.

She was holding Debbie, feeding her, and a new nurse, Amy, was feeding Jilly, holding her well away from her and talking to her in a distanced manner. Nurse Nancy talked about all the screaming, telling Debbie off, but saying that it was not really her fault The nurses seemed angry and exasperated. Jilly began to scream. The nurse put her down, and Jilly became frantic. Nurse Jean picked her up, got a sling, and asked me and Susan, the speech therapist, to help her put Jilly into it. We did, and she laughed, saying that it took three people to look after her. Jilly was instantly quietened. Nurse Jean got on with looking after the other babies, with Jilly strapped to her front.

The babies were blamed for the situation, although there was some recognition that they were not really to blame. It was some weeks before people would talk to me openly about their worries about Jilly's possible HIV status, but I think that we can see here how

Jilly was kept at a distance, both physically and mentally. Nurses said that they just had to follow ordinary guidelines, but these did not allow for the fear and horror that people were feeling that a baby might be carrying this disease. Nurses were also very frightened that as father did not realize that mother was ill and that they could not tell him because the couple were not married, he might become very angry with them when he did find out. Some nurses even felt that he might come with a gun. So the feelings around Jilly were very raw. Nurse Jean, a mother herself, was confident in recognizing Jilly's needs, but she seemed to want some emotional support in strapping her on, perhaps acknowledging that one needs all the internal resources one can muster in looking after a baby as persecuted as Jilly. The following day I came into the Nursery:

> Nurse Jean was about to put Jilly into the sling but could not because Debbie was screaming. She was torn in two directions and gave Jilly to me. It was unusual for me to hold the babies, as my job was to observe and think about what was going on; it was a sign of how fraught the nursery was that I was used in this way. Nurse Jean gave me the dummy, which I gave to Jilly, who had a fight with it, wanting it and not wanting it. She was screaming and writhing, and I felt tremendously incompetent. I put her up on my shoulder, and she quietened. She was facing outwards, and I could not see what she was doing, but she was hot and wet on my shoulder—sucking her hand, or was it the overall that I had been given to put on? She was awake and moving, restless but quiet. Sometimes she got disturbed, and I would rock her or pat her. Whatever position calmed her did not last for long. I put her on my lap and she began to scream: the sound was like sandpaper—rough and coarse. I put her on my shoulder and walked with her, and she was quiet, although moving around and trying to find a comfortable place. Then she began crying frantically. I wondered where the dummy was. I tried this and that, but she cried—awful screaming—legs and arms drawn in and her face red. A nurse gave me a dummy, which I held in for Jilly, and she calmed down immediately. She closed her eyes and nestled into me. She sucked

and rested, her hands clasped together. I watched her very intently while holding the dummy firmly in her mouth. She sucked and stopped, sucked and stopped—her face mostly clear but occasionally crumpling, but not succumbing to disintegration. When she became disturbed, I rocked her while holding the dummy in, and she quietened. I reflected on what constant minute-by-minute care she needed. She began struggling on the dummy, not wanting it but frantic without it. I devised a strategy of taking it away for a second and then returning it, my idea being that she felt it had to be decontaminated, but that she needed it back quickly. This seemed to work, and we struggled on. Gradually she fell into a deepish sleep. Any bit of peace had to be welcomed for itself rather than as a promise of a period of calm. Soon I put her down, and she lay just as I placed her, without her dummy.

I wondered why Jilly was so constantly on the move. It seemed to me that whatever was good very quickly became bad, but I also thought that perhaps stillness felt like emptiness and had to be avoided, that constant movement kept terror at bay. Her scream was awful and sounded as if she were in hell. One way she seemed to be able to get rid of some of the horror was through her mouth. She seemed to put anxiety into the dummy and to need to get rid of it, but then needed it back to take the next lot. It seemed to me that at this time the dummy was very useful to her.

The following week I went to see Jilly, who was now 5 weeks old.

She was crying, and Nurse Harriet picked her up. She carried her on her left arm, with Jilly's head on it and her left arm down under Harriet's arm and her right arm on Harriet's arm. Both Jilly's hands were in fists. Her eyes were open, and Harriet was jiggling her. She looked around, and Harriet held her firmly, with hands clasped between her legs. Harriet talked to other parents, holding and jiggling Jilly all the time. Jilly looked around, her eyes closed and opened, closed and opened. Her left hand opened. Her eyes closed, her left hand curled, and she went to sleep. Harriet went to put a dummy into

Debbie's mouth because she was crying. Jilly woke up, and her hands went into fists. As Debbie stopped crying, Jilly's eyes closed, and her hands hung down.

Jilly yawned, and Harriet tried to give her a dummy. But she did not want it, and Harriet took it away. Jilly then opened her mouth several times. Her eyes were open, and her hands were in fists. She looked around, moving her hands and opening her mouth. She seemed perhaps to be looking for something, perhaps to be yawning. Then she was crying, and Harriet very gently talked to her and put her over her shoulder. Then she began screaming.

Nurse Harriet held her sideways and took off her babygro, saying that she was boiling. She cried less frantically, quietened a little, and then cried more. Debbie began to cry and Nurse Harriet looked perplexed about which baby to go to. I offered to hold Jilly and immediately noticed how smelly she was. I tried to put this out of my mind, but I could not understand why Nurse Harriet, who, I thought, was an excellent nurse, had not changed her. But I also felt the brunt of Nurse Harriet's irritability as she asked me what I would do with these observations. I said that I wanted to write something about withdrawing babies. She brightened up and said yes, I should write about what it feels like. I asked her whether she meant the babies or the nurses, and she said what the nurses feel like doing: throwing the babies out the window.

So I—or, rather, Jilly—was left with this dirty nappy, and I did not feel as if I could say anything. I tried Jilly over my shoulder, on my lap, walking, with a dummy, without. And she just screamed and screamed, sometimes a little less, but usually more, and at one point so that she could hardly breathe, and I thought that she might die, and I would stand guilty. I felt that there was general appreciation of the fact that I was having such a hard time; one or two of the nurses grinned. I gave her back to Harriet, who said that she was dirty, and dismissed it. I plucked up the courage to say that perhaps Jilly did mind. She put her in her cot and undid her nappy. She remarked that she had the runs. Jilly stopped crying, and they looked at each

other. Harriet spoke sweetly to her as she cleaned her up, saying that she did not like having a dirty nappy, did she, and that
that was better, was it not, and that she would dry her now. But
then another nurse came over, the two nurses started talking,
and the moment of connection was lost. Jilly became upset, but
in a more controlled way. Harriet said to her that she couldn't
stay with her . . . she just couldn't. She wrapped her in a sheet,
saying that sometimes she liked this and sometimes she did
not, but that anyway she liked to have her hands out. Jilly
was screaming, and Harriet lay her on her tummy. Jilly worked
herself right up against the right-hand corner of the cot. I came
back later, and she was quiet, squashed up in the corner.
Harriet had put a sheet over the cot to protect her from the light
and noise.

Jilly had the runs and at first Nurse Harriet seemed reluctant to
clear up the mess. When she did, there were a few moments of
intimacy between her and Jilly. I think that the nurses were feeling
that Jilly was abandoned to them, but particularly to Harriet. At
times her mother was so ill that she was hospitalized. There was an
atmosphere of misery and blame. I certainly felt useless—unable to
comfort Jilly—and I imagine that that was often how the nurses
were feeling. It was very hard to bear Jilly's inconsolability—and
to see it as such and not to be tormented by it. I think that Jilly
was living in a very frightening place—perhaps the jiggling that
calmed her pushed the fear and pain out of her mind. When
Harriet offered her the dummy, it seemed both to be not what she
wanted and to remind her that there was something that she did
want. This was a very fragmented world, where any meaning ran
away, much like Jilly's insides did; so it was hard for the nurses to
hold on to what they knew—that is, that babies tend not to like
dirty nappies and want to keep their carer's attention once they
have got it. Jilly banged herself right up in the corner of her cot—
maybe with some hope of escaping from her tormentors. Nurse
Harriet put the sheet over her to give her some peace from so
much stimulation, but also maybe to protect Jilly from her murderous impulses towards her. She had asked me what I did with the
observations and clearly talked about murderousness. I thought
the issue here was who would recognize and bear the nurses'

feelings—provide a nappy, as it were, so that these feelings did not have to run away and be acted out.

That same week I went to see Jilly again. I had noticed that nurses were discussing her more: what ways did she like to lie, did swaddling help, did she like her arms in or out, her legs free or swaddled? On this occasion it was midday and I was told that she had been screaming all morning.

I saw that a senior nurse had been feeding her. She was very firmly wrapped up, with her arms in, and put lying on her right side. She had her eyes closed and was very still. She wriggled a little, made some sucking movements, and dribbled some milk. She moved and made a little noise and was still. She shrugged a little, pursed her lips, and fluttered her eyelids. She made a little movement of her head and then her lips. She made a little noise, wriggled, and coughed. She made more noises. Her mouth was open, and her tongue was moving inside her mouth.

This observation continued, with Jilly's eyes opening and looking around, and her mouth opening and her tongue moving inside it. I was struck by the big void of her mouth and her tongue inside.

She began wriggling more inside the swaddling, and this sometimes turned into struggling: her left foot kicked out of the sheet, and her arms seemed to be trying to get out. Her mouth opened, and again I could see her tongue inside. She moved the sheet off with her arms. She put her mouth up against the sheet and mouthed it. She took her head away from the sheet and then back. She put the sheet over her face and then moved it away. Then she got completely free from the sheet. She seemed quite calm. She stretched and opened her eyes very wide. Her arms and legs gyrated, and she hiccoughed. She was looking towards me but not into my eyes. She looked over towards a crying baby, and her leg and arm movements grew less. She was sucking. Her tongue went out, and she was making little noises. She stretched her arms up above her and then back down. Then she was gyrating. She looked towards the light. She looked towards me. She stretched her right hand out in her field of vision. Then looked up to another light in the ceiling.

Then back towards me. Then back to the first light. Then back towards me. Her mouth was open, and her tongue was out. She looked at me, hiccoughed, and looked away to the left side. Then up to the first light. Her hands went down for a second and then up to shoulder level in little loose fists. She was hiccoughing. Her left index finger went to the thumb and went towards her mouth and away. She made little noises. Again her finger and thumb went to her mouth.

I was intrigued. It seemed to me to be the first time that I had seen Jilly awake and exploring her world. The nurse who had fed her was someone quietly confident, who knew her own mind, and there was that look about the way Jilly was lying in her cot. She seemed safely held, and from that base she could go exploring. At first I felt struck by this cavernous hole of her mouth and felt that it did not have a proper grip, and that likewise her eyes would look in a direction but not fix. But this gradually changed as the mouth seemed to focus more around the tongue, which became not just something in the mouth, but something that could move and go in and out. She seemed to struggle out of her sheet a bit like a moth out of the chrysalis, and she could then put her mouth to the sheet and then the sheet to her mouth. She seemed to be gaining some mastery over her world, going after what she wanted, but also able to bring it to her—all this with a new degree of calm. This observation began with a discovery of security. Perhaps we need this before we can begin to have a sense of separateness and therefore of self. In this observation Jilly did something. She pulled the sheet away and back—she achieved something rather than having something done to her. Perhaps we see here the precursors of a separate existence. And then this exploration with her mouth and what goes into it seems to remind her that there is a world out there and she looks towards the light, towards her fist and then to the person sitting with her looking at her. She then goes on a voyage, from the lights that she used to stare at when she was being fed to the person, backwards and forwards, as if getting to know the path. Then she makes the connection between her thumb and index finger going to her mouth and away. This is something we see babies in the intensive nursery struggle to do, and here we see Jilly only achieve it at around 6 weeks, but it is very moving to see her manage it. I think that she had at last been able to make these basic connections against the blast and fragmentation of her withdrawal. She had to work hard to overcome the experience of her extra-uterine life and presumably her intra-uterine life too.

Five days later I went to see Jilly. She was now 7 weeks old. The nurse in charge said that she was a bit better. This is what I saw:

Jilly was lying on her tummy; her head was to the right, and her right hand was to her mouth. She was well tucked in. I was struck by how much bigger she looked; it was five days since I had seen her. She was rather still, lightly sucking on her hand. She stretched slightly and sucked the side of her hand. Then her mouth opened on her hand, and moved on it, closing. Her mouth opened, and her hand was against her lower lip. Her eyes looked as if they were about to open. Her hand was very gently against her lower lip. Her top lip pursed. Her lower lip sucked. Her top lip pursed. Her hand moved about half an inch away from her mouth. She was sucking, and her hand moved slightly. Her lower lip—perhaps really her chin—was sucking, and then her top lip pursed. Her hand moved almost imperceptibly. Then there was stronger sucking of her jaw. Her eyes flickered and her eyebrows went up as if her eyes were going to open. Her mouth pulled back. Her lips closed very quickly, and there was some movement round her eyes. Her thumb moved and was almost touching her lower lip and then was touching it. Her top lip moved, and then her bottom lip sucked. . . . Her hand moved and touched her bottom lip very gently. Her lips came together for a second, and then her tongue came out between them. Her mouth was closing and opening a little, with her tongue moving around inside. She moved her face into the sheet, nuzzling. Then she rested with her mouth open, her hand away from her mouth and her fingers curled underneath. She was still, and her mouth was in a triangle. She sucked and pulled her mouth back.

I was astonished by this observation: by the disparate movements of her upper and lower lips. I tried to move my lips not in unison and found it very difficult to do anything approaching what Jilly was doing. This is how I made sense of it for myself. Earlier in

Jilly's life I had noticed how she would go for the bottle and then fight against it. I thought that whatever was good quickly became bad. But also maybe there was a fight within her between going for what she needed and turning away from it. One might think of this as a healthy turning towards and a perverse turning away. Of course, this is all complicated for Jilly because her experience is so filled with ambiguity. Presumably even *in utero* she suffered the hell of withdrawal and the relief of the drug. Then, in the first few weeks, she had cycles of the relief of the methadone and then the hell of the lack of it. So the drug, which caused her misery, also gave her relief from it. One nurse told me that she never struggled against the methadone, even at the beginning. But the bottle— what I would see as the representative of maternity, comfort, nourishment, healthy dependency, the growing recognition of some source outside that she could relate to—was something she often fought against. So early on she suffered from this terrible ambiguity. In this observation she seemed to have found a remarkable way of effecting a useful split. It seemed that the bottom lip, supported by her jaw, could get on with expressing a healthy wish to turn to nourishment and to suck. The top lip, the purser, expressed the wish to turn away—the wish that we would expect to find in a more developed form as contempt or even perversion. With Jilly, this seemed a very helpful split, lifting her conflict to a more expressive symbolic sphere. All of this seemed to happen under the gentle aegis of her hand, which gently came and went and which touched and supported her bottom lip. The internal world in which she was living seemed to be improving along with improvement in the external world of the nursery.

Susan, the speech and language therapist, and I decided that we would show a video of Jilly to the unit. We had meetings that anyone from the NICU was welcome to attend. In these meetings we would show quite small clips of video in sequence and stop to discuss what we had seen. We asked participants to observe the baby, the environment, and their own feelings in response to watching the clip, all in the service of trying to come to a better understanding of what was going on. When we began these meetings, it was in an attempt to present a NIDCAP[1] point of view, followed by the speech therapist and my more psychoanalytic baby-observation view. We wanted to show Jilly partly because she was having such a hard time but also because we saw what an emotional toll she took on the nurses. We hoped that by offering a place to discuss all this away from the tension of the nursery, we might be helping to improve the situation. This meeting in the autumn was attended by a group of nurses, a play specialist, Susan, and myself. We showed a clip of Jilly crying and then being held by the play specialist.

In the discussion Nurse Shirley said that she thought that Jilly felt that she had something very bad inside her and that she was trying to get rid of it. We talked about how she was rubbing her legs together as if trying to scrape something off them. The play specialist said that adult addicts had told her that they felt as if they were crawling with ants. She added that Jilly did not like being stroked gently, she liked firm handling. It was remarked that she pushed herself up against the hard surface of the cot, that it seemed that she liked to come up against something. It is difficult for nurses to allow this to happen, as they would naturally position a baby in the middle of the cot. Nurse Rosie said that she was only speaking personally—and I interrupted her to say that that was all that any of us could do, that we can all only use our own thoughts and experience—but, she said, she could not bear the sound of the play specialist's music; there were the babies crying, the monitors were going off, and then there was this music—it was too much, you felt bombarded. Then everyone talked about feeling irritable. The play specialist said that you couldn't be of any use to Jilly when you were irritated—she had felt like that the other day, and she had had to leave the room for five minutes to recover, otherwise she would upset Jilly. I said that I thought we might think of it the other way round—that we pick up some of Jilly's feelings, so that by examining our own feelings, we can learn something about Jilly's feelings. I thought that perhaps Jilly, too, felt bombarded when addressed by too many sensations at once—perhaps she, too, could only concentrate on one thing at a time. The nurses discussed this and their own irritability. I said that the play specialist had left the room to recover and that I wondered what the nurses did by way of relief; that part of the point of this meeting was to discuss these things in the effort to recover. This led on to a discussion about whether there could be just one nurse for a baby like Jilly, so that you did not feel all the time that you should be with another baby. It was generally recognized that this was a good idea, but it was thought that the other mothers might be jealous. Also, it was felt that it would not work, because if Jilly was quiet, you would feel you had to help with the other babies. This brought us on to the topic of mothers. Nurse Joanna said that Jilly would usually settle when her mother came in. The other nurses hotly disagreed, saying that when her mother came in, they had already calmed Jilly. Joanna stuck to her view that Jilly settled best for her mother.

It seems to me that this discussion was very important. Nurse Shirley said clearly that Jilly feels as if she has something bad inside, and that by crying she is trying to get rid of it. There is a question about how when we feel bad we can get rid of it—evacuate it, scrape it off. Also there is a recognition of her need for something firm outside to get security from in this nightmare. The image of ants crawling all over one is vivid and makes one wonder about Jilly's experience of her skin. Perhaps it did not feel like an integrated membrane that held her together, but as something horrible in itself. Certainly her nappy rash was very bad and prolonged and must have been painful.

As the discussion went on, Nurse Rosie felt safe enough to voice her own feelings of discomfort and her anger with the play specialist for aggravating this. The question then arises whether we can hold on to these feelings and use them to understand what is going on or whether we, too, have to get rid of them. Can we cope with these feelings by accepting them and thinking about them, being interested in them rather than just pushing them out? It is useful to acknowledge how irritable staff can get with one another, and this can then be seen as part of the whole picture and not be perpetuated as personal dislike. It was then agreed that a baby needs one or two caretakers: people who know her intimately, help her to make sense of her world, and provide continuity. This quite logically led us on to thoughts of her mother, who would be the natural person to fulfil this job. Quite a hot dispute followed about who could get Jilly to settle.

There is a telling scene in Dennis Potter's *Blue Remembered Hills*, where the grown-up little girls quarrel about who is going to be mother, and in the tussle the baby doll gets thrown on the ground. When a baby is very difficult, like Jilly, she can be thought of as a rubbish baby that nobody wants to look after; but once she becomes the focus of some interest, I think our little-girl feelings of who is the best mother can be aroused, so that we can become competitive with the mother and with each other—who is best with her, who understands her better, and so on. Particularly where the baby has suffered from the mother's behaviour, it is hard to think that Jilly might have a real and important link with her mother. When Jilly was tiny, she hated having her nappy changed. This was something that the nurses thought about a lot, partly from watching the video—how they could do it in a way that upset her less. Then she began to like having her nappy changed. I think that she came to feel relieved to have the dirty nappy taken away and dealt with and to be cleaned up by a confident nurse who often talked to her while doing this, so that this was not just a matter of changing her nappy but also of processing and giving words to her feelings. In the same way, I think, unit staff have messy feelings about the babies, and these need a place where they can be articulated with tact and kindness. In this meeting they turned out to be feelings of some general interest, which can help us, and which, when seen as having a legitimate place, are less in danger of suddenly exploding.

At around 7 or 8 weeks Jilly seemed to become more dependent on those around her. Once, when I held the dummy in for her, I spoke to someone else, and her hand flew onto my hand and held it in place with tremendous force. She would also clutch on to a finger, seemingly for security. Nurse Rosie told me that Jilly wanted to be held all the time. I wondered if the meaning of this had changed somewhat. Earlier she had wanted continual movement, perhaps to keep nightmarish sensations at bay; now she had some idea of something that at times took the torture away, something that could help, and she did not want to lose this. She was discussed a lot on the unit, and people would boast that she had smiled at or talked to them. In the middle of the horror, people seemed to be getting glimpses of an ordinary, beautiful baby.

I went to see Jilly when she was 9 weeks old. The nurses said that she had been all over the place for days and that she was still on methadone.

The lights were low, and Jilly was in the pram. She was looking to her left, and the dummy was held in by her right hand. Her left hand was in a fist, held out towards the wall of the pram. She looked very peaceful and was breathing evenly. She was in a deep sleep, undisturbed by all the noise around her. She made the smallest movement on her dummy and with her left hand. She scarcely moved for twenty minutes. Meanwhile I found myself assailed by the most paranoid and upsetting thoughts. These gradually became very sad. Jilly moved, stretched, and her dummy fell out. She seemed to be looking for it. I gave it to her, and gradually she accepted it, feeling my hand with her hands. Her hands then came together, went apart, came together again. Then she kicked the blanket off. She looked around as if she was expecting something. She looked at me, and I spoke to her. She smiled at me. She was looking and smiling; she had her mouth open, and her tongue was going in and out. Whenever I spoke to her, she broke into radiant smiles. I had to leave, and she cried.

I wondered if I were carrying the feelings of misery and paranoia, while Jilly slept in peace. But I also thought about her pre- and postnatal experience, when she was invaded both by the drug and by the lack of it. I thought that she might have felt as if she had no boundaries, as if she were wide open to whatever came her way. I thought that now she might be feeling more separate, to have got more of a skin, so that the feelings that were mine were mine, and she did not have to be involved in them. Perhaps she had developed some defences to protect her from the outside. Then, when she awoke, she could be happy to see this person, who responded in tune with her need, who spoke to her and thought about her, so now there could be a meeting.

At that time Susan and I had another video session. We showed a track of Jilly being bathed by Joanna. Several nurses attended. In the film Jilly was screaming, and whatever Joanna did seemed to make no difference. One participant asked whether we thought that Jilly was ill with HIV—how could withdrawal go on for so long—or was it that she had got used to crying, that this was all she knew? Nurse Harriet said that she was no longer comforted by her mother. Someone replied that they were glad, because the mother would now know what she was taking on. But Harriet thought with despair that Jilly would then not even have her mother to comfort her. This led to a general worry about how mother would ever manage at home. The nurses said that they could not bear the screaming, even though they only had to put up with it for a shift. Also, mother was an addict and so would have less patience. Someone added that she did not have somewhere like here to come to talk about Jilly and her own feelings. We looked at some more video, where Joanna took off Jilly's nappy and put her into the bath. Jilly screamed throughout. Joanna said "Oh, Jilly, you are so miserable", as if she, too, might cry. As Joanna swooshed the water around her and spoke to her, saying that now she felt safe and comfortable, Jilly stopped crying. She put her hand down towards her raw nappy area. She began crying, and Joanna put her on her tummy over her arm.

There was a discussion about how we can know what babies are feeling—that they surely do not have concepts that we have. People talked about very primitive sensations, such as falling or turning to liquid (going down the plug hole). We talked about how, when you can give words to feelings or tell a story around them, they are less frightening, so Jilly was in a more unprotected state than we are.

We thought about the comfort that Jilly got from the water. But one nurse pointed out that even when she stopped crying, her hands were clenched. We noticed that once she was over Joanna's arm in the water, her cry had quite a different quality—it was more of a complaint, like when you go home and whinge about how dreadful the day has been. Harriet said that the frantic cry sounded like "Get me out of this." I thought that what was so awful about it was that there was no belief that there was someone there, whereas the complaint was to someone.

The nurses began talking about how they might have looked after Jilly better. Would a more isolated room, with less stimulation, have been preferable? Others were worried that she would then have been left too much on her own. They talked about her need for darkness and to be wrapped up. Harriet said that if they tried isolation with another baby and he did better, they would never know if it actually was a better method or if this baby was less ill.

We watched more video of Joanna trying to feed Jilly. She kept the bottle in her mouth, although Jilly was screaming. One nurse laughed and said "You will take this bottle!" People felt sympathy for the nurse but thought that she had persisted for too long. We agreed that one just longed for Jilly's mouth to close around the teat. We talked about how hard it was to watch the video. Harriet said that she just comforted herself with the thought that Jilly would remember none of this. This started a by now familiar argument between those who agreed with that and those who did not. One nurse put it that she would not remember it, but she would be shaped by it. Another said that we generally think that the first few weeks of life are important, so they must be for Jilly too. They acknowledged ruefully how keen they were to hand her on to someone else and how numerous were those she was handled by as a result.

One nurse then said that she thought that the mother was evil. How could these addicts do these things? The mothers talked about how awful withdrawal was, without thinking what they were putting the babies through. Another nurse said that Debbie's father seemed proud of the methadone and the withdrawal, as if it made them special. They talked about AIDS and the risks and the split condom that mother said had produced Jilly. They laughed a little and said how boring their lives were. As they left, one nurse said how brilliant these sessions were.

Susan and I hoped that these sessions would give rise to real improvements in the care of the babies and she was very good at holding on to this aim and put up notes over a baby's cot with suggestions about practice. We also hoped that by giving the staff a space to reflect on their own observations, they would not only be given the chance to have practical ideas, but these would have sprung from thinking about the baby's experience. This session had begun with concern for Jilly and her mother. We talked about the philosophical problem of knowing about anyone else's experience and how this was even more difficult with a baby. To help our imagination, we had to rely on our most primitive fears, and we knew that Jilly would be even more vulnerable than most of us because of her immaturity. The nurses seemed to admit to their own feelings of vulnerability and to have an imaginative discussion about Jilly's chronic crying. In the same way, Joanna had coped with her sadness and had gone on to comfort Jilly. But the thought that the care could have been better was a very painful one. Feelings were raw, and perhaps in response there was a wish to put Jilly in isolation—a wish that the group managed to resist. Then the torment of seeing Jilly unable to be comforted broke out in anxieties about what all this was doing to Jilly: would she be able to get away from it, or would she be stuck with this nightmare forever? I was struck by how one of the most sensitive nurses clung to the view that all this was just for the moment and would pass without a trace. Perhaps any other view was too distressing for her and, indeed, for most of us. There was a wish at this point to shift the blame on to mother and, more generally, on to addicts.

"Where do babies come from?" is a very common childhood question and maybe it is not just about the mechanics of inter-course but about what sort of union a baby does come from. I think that unconsciously such thoughts affect us all. With Jilly in the unit, perhaps we entertained an idea that she was the product of a murderous intercourse, where any number of people might, conse-quently, have become infected—that she was the product of a split condom, a sort of bad joke, and perhaps to be thrown away, like an old used condom. Furthermore, she had the nerve to prefer her mother, allowing her to settle her when the nurses could not—surely a sign of her bad taste, to choose this mother over the nurses! Gradually the mother in this woman had to be recognized and staff became concerned about her, and about father, who was something more than a potential gunman.

At the beginning of December, Jilly came off her methadone, and she left the unit quite suddenly—or so it seemed to me. I saw her on a Thursday, and when I came in the following Tuesday, she had left. I felt bereft. Her corner of the Nursery looked terribly empty. I continue to wonder how she is and what her life will be like.

Note

1. NIDCAP (Neonatal Individualised Development Care and Assessment Pro-gramme) is a system of intervention that has encouraged a move away from cares being clustered together and carried out on the baby at a prescribed time. Instead, the baby is viewed as an individual who has his own timetable for

cares. In addition, this neuro-developmental approach acknowledges that the baby has a threshold of sensitivity for interventions, together with his own unique repertoire of self-coping strategies. The in-depth NIDCAP observation records the baby's behaviour before, during and after care. The resulting profile of the baby allows appreciation of the synchronicity, stability and fragility of the baby's emerging systems. These systems are the autonomic and motor systems, together with the baby's self-regulatory system. The observations identify the baby's levels of stress and competence during procedures. Recommendations are then given to parents and carers, which aim to facilitate stability by supporting the baby's own self regulatory behaviours. These include modifications to positioning, the nursery environment and carer approach during procedures. [I am grateful to Gillian Kennedy, a speech and language therapist, for this account.]

CHAPTER ELEVEN

Vicissitudes of life on a neonatal unit

"If you don't talk about it, you don't know it's bad."

Nurse on the NICU in 2002

"Doing" staff support is a fairly complex enterprise. It is an attempt to influence the culture and atmosphere of the unit—trying to keep people in mind as individuals and to keep the babies as the clear focus of our work.

When staff complain about the problems that arise recurrently on the unit, I sometimes say that maintaining good working conditions is a bit like doing housework: it is never finished. No sooner have you done it than it is time to do it again, and in some way one needs to be conscious of it all the time. One smart SHO replied to this that one could get a cleaner; I answered that that was Dr Gibbons's and my job. In the past, I had run a junior doctors' weekly support meeting, and, together, Dr Gibbons and I ran a weekly staff support meeting for any staff on the unit. In general, this was attended by nurses, but occasionally doctors came, and consultants, if they were invited. We also have a monthly paediatric consultants' meeting attended by five of the six consultants, as described in chapter 9. In addition, staff are welcome to come and see either of us individually. They tend to see me. A nurse or doctor may be finding that work on the unit is disturbing their personal life—they may be having trouble conceiving, or it may be difficult to be pregnant and to be looking after these small babies. Junior doctors may find it particularly difficult to return to work after having had a baby: one young woman told me, in tears, that whenever she was taking blood from a baby, she saw her own baby's face. Sometimes there are political or professional aspects to all of these issues. Our task is to listen and to help people to elucidate their feelings and thereby be clearer about what they want for themselves and clearer about what is going on among themselves. From time to time morale on the unit becomes low, and it is sometimes difficult to pinpoint why. It will be obvious from previous chapters what some of the reasons might be: for instance, a baby might be very ill or might be dying, or parents may be having a very hard time. But sometimes the problems are among the staff. At the time when I was working on this book, the atmosphere on the unit seemed particularly bad. But when I looked back over my years of working on the unit, I realized that the situation was not so unusual. I decided to write about one of these low troughs.

When things are difficult, it is easy to adopt some prelapsarian view: that there was a time when everything on the unit was wonderful. In fact, it has always had its problems, which tend to go in cycles of rather good functioning and conflict. It can be hard to get hold of what is going on at times of conflict, because so many strands are involved. As I have reiterated throughout this book, it is always hard to keep the babies as the main focus of work. In most cases they have come too early, so they are immature and vulnerable. They often threaten to terrify us because they may suddenly die or, after much painstaking work, end up as very damaged children. This is perhaps the most frequent unspoken thought on the unit: that perhaps all of this work and pain is misspent—perhaps the enterprise is even morally wrong. Only the doctors and nurses know in graphic detail what pain the babies go through in the first few days and weeks. The parents are often shielded from this. In a staff support meeting after 11 September, one nurse said that what we do to the babies in the first few hours, particularly intubation, is like Armageddon. She was associating the shock of the impact of the planes into the twin towers with what the babies undergo. The group went on to think about how hard it is to imagine, for instance, the terror of the people in the planes, or the terror of the people in the towers, and this led it on to thinking about how hard it is to imagine what the babies' experience amounts to—and that when you begin to think about it, it is sickening. This was said by a good and sensitive nurse with a child of her own, and for her to say this took courage; nobody could comment on it until much later in the meeting. Many of the babies described in the previous chapters go to very difficult families; sometimes their mother does not want them, sometimes a drug-addicted mother cannot appreciate the experience of withdrawal the baby has undergone. Mothers are often without a supportive partner or friends, and they may be deprived of support from their own mothers. Also, many families are immigrants, refugees, or asylum-seekers. The loss of a full-term pregnancy may be part of a picture of loss—of family, of house, of country: living in an alien culture, where they may not understand the language. We know that women experiencing these kinds of losses are more likely to give birth prematurely. We also have mothers coming to us from the local women's prison. Whatever difficulties the mothers and babies come with—and in the twelve years that I have worked on the unit, these seem to get ever more diverse and serious—this new experience, an early birth, is a fresh defeat for them. The birth itself is often a terrible shock, coming out of the blue, or it may have happened after weeks of trying to hold on to the baby. I have sometimes sat on the antenatal ward with a mother who is in this state and is finding it hard to be so tied to the vagaries of her body, lying down, trying to hold on to her baby and postpone labour for weeks. Mothers with multiple pregnancies have particular problems: one mother went on to 28 weeks' gestation with one live twin inside and one twin that had been dead for 7 weeks. So the patient group is very diverse and needy.

The unit has been the subject of planning blight for some time. There are plans to merge with two other large hospitals nearby, which I shall call Hospital C and Hospital D. Nurses feel that they are not given clear information about what stage these plans have reached. I think there is a lack of understanding in management that we need to feel identified with where we work—that we need to put down roots and feel at home in this place, that it is important to us that we have a particular culture at work, which may not be better or worse than in other places but is ours. This may have a competitive or rivalrous quality, but it also involves a sense of pride. There has definitely been a rivalry between these hospitals in the past. On the whole, nurses have come from Hospital C to our hospital to learn; now the balance has changed, and the flow is veering in the other direction. So there is a question of how people are to think about a merger. In many ways this is not so difficult for doctors. They are already quite used to changing hospitals—it is one of the hazards of their work that they move frequently, and it becomes difficult to put down roots. But nurses tend to live nearby, with their children at local nurseries and schools. They are worried about disruption if they have to move to another location for their work. They are reassured that they will all have work after the merger, which is clearly the case since there is such a shortage of nurses in London. But they do not really believe this. The upheaval could be managed if we got on with it—but at the time of writing it has dragged on for years, often with a sense that something is going to happen. Gradually, with no political decisions and no management directives, nurses begin to distance themselves from their place of work, to care less about it, and their ability to give stability to the mothers and babies wears down. They can feel quite hostile to the mothers, thinking that they get an unfair amount of consideration while they, the nurses, are overlooked or treated badly.

Dr Gibbons and I decided to amalgamate the two weekly staff meetings—that is, the junior doctors' group and the general staff group. We thought that it would be good for doctors and nurses to be talking to each other in a weekly meeting. The argument for separate meetings was that the junior doctors are so vulnerable that they need a private place to talk, where they do not have to be putting on an image of being able to cope with everything and anything. The doctors themselves were keen for the amalgamation, feeling that although some privacy was good at first, a few weeks into the job it would be good to be talking more to nurses. So, having discussed this for a few months, we made the change. Initially nurses attended less, perhaps feeling that they were no longer responsible for the meetings or maybe feeling inhibited by the presence of the doctors. After several months both doctors and nurses were attending, and there was an opportunity for the combined discussions that we had hoped for.

Staff support has its intrinsic difficulty. Junior staff, both doctors and nurses, need permission from their seniors to attend. There are usually some defensive thoughts that it is pathetic to want support, that it is stronger to get on with the work and let weaker brethren attend. A masochistic or heroic attitude, whichever it is, arises where one can work without food, or even without peeing! Staff support threatens such self-idealization, so people need clear encouragement, even instructions, to come. The consultant paediatricians think that the meetings are essential, and they tell the new SHOs so. But the views of the registrars vary. Some understand the point of the meetings and come without difficulty, thus enabling their juniors to come. Others, more numerous, find it threatening and, subtly or not so subtly, take their juniors away. They have a legitimate task: to look after their juniors, to weld them into a team—and sometimes this is done in a jocular way that undermines attention to problematic feelings. Given the nature of the work, one can understand the pull of such an attitude. But it is disastrous for the unit and the quality of the work. It leads to an overall denial of feeling and to poorer service for the mothers and babies. Registrars are on the unit for four months and SHOs for six, so we may just be establishing good contact when it is time for them to move. The nurses, too, need to be encouraged to attend. They have asked us to invite them each week, to go through the nurseries telling them to come, so that they can feel that they are allowed to. At this time the nurse manager would not actively support the meetings, saying that people were adults and could get their support where they wished. She did not appreciate that staff need to be led towards it—that if, for instance, a baby has died, staff need to be advised to come to a meeting. So it is sometimes a problem to get staff to come to meetings, but every week someone comes and usually there are quite a few.

A few months after we amalgamated the groups, we gradually became aware of disquiet among the nurses. This was kept remarkably well hidden from us, and most attempts we made to talk about it were stonewalled. However, nurses did say that work was hell, so horrible that they did not want to come to work. At that time it was said that this discontent was among the middle-grade staff, who had criticisms of the senior staff. One nurse said that when you came in, you looked to see who you were working with, and your heart might sink. There were several occasions when staff talked to us more openly, but in general over the summer we felt impotent. What we noticed was a recurring situation where the problems were alluded to, but it was hard for us to decipher the hints and to be of much use. We felt that there was an investment in maintaining an atmosphere of intrigue and hatred, stirring it and leaving us impotent in the face of it. It was generally recognized that staff morale was very low. There were worries about mergers, and several nurses left, which entailed an even greater shortage. This became so severe that the intermediate nursery had to be closed. The unit became closed to outside admissions, and there was even talk about it being closed down altogether. This fuelled thoughts that it had gone from a strong position to being the weakest of the three units and that it would be swallowed up.

During these months there was a plan to make a booklet for each baby who was going to foster care and then to adoption in order to provide that baby's history on the unit. This sprang from a sense that these children do not have anyone to carry their early history for them and that they might like—even need—in later life to know more about what had happened to them. This eventually produced quite a storm, since people's idea of what was appropriate varied considerably. The nurses produced a book of photographs for a particular baby. This failed to capture in any way the traumatic early time that this baby had lived through. It had been totally forgotten or perhaps suppressed that at first the nurses had not liked this baby. Gradually he had swung from being hated to becoming the unit mascot. The photograph book included captions of an ironic and flirtatious kind attributed to the baby. It seemed to me that all this completely missed the point of what was required. The newly appointed additional child psychotherapist working on the unit wrote a letter, to be included in the photograph album, about some early difficulties the baby had lived through. Some doctors as well as some nurses objected, believing that it was better for the person concerned never to know what he had experienced. I believed that in his later life that person might have features that would make more sense if he knew what these first weeks had been like. There was a stormy meeting to discuss these issues. The social workers claimed that they write a history and that that goes into the information that the person can eventually have available. My query was that this would only provide information of a very general nature, saying that he had been in intensive care for so many weeks, and would give no idea of what life had really been like. I thought that accounts of early experience by the speech and language therapist and the child psychotherapist could usefully be added to the social workers' reports. I believed this from past experience acquired in supervising child psychotherapists' work with young people who had had a NICU experience and because I felt that some knowledge of what that baby had gone through was very useful, both to the young person and to the therapist. The consultant paediatrician said that a book of photos of an unembarrassing kind might be nice for the child and his new family, but that we should be thinking also about making available information that would help the grown child and his family make links between his behaviour or thoughts and his early experience. It was agreed that the social workers would show us an example of what they do and that we would meet again. This did not happen. I felt that in this mood the nurses had not been able to bear anything but a very idealized image of themselves. It also seemed that, with the captions to the photographs, a flirtatious sexuality was being used to defend themselves from the reality of this baby's experience and from their own hatred of him.

As related in previous chapters, for many years I had sometimes organized a meeting first with one speech therapist and then with another, in which we showed a sequence of small video clips of a particular baby and then paused to discuss what we had seen and how we felt about it. All members of staff were invited. The original speech therapist who had gone on to work at Hospital D accepted my invitation to do a series of these meetings with me first at our hospital and then at hers. We decided to invite the other NICU child psychotherapist and speech therapist to join us in this. Together, we ran a series of meetings over the autumn term. My thought was to try to get the emphasis away from the personal and political agitations and back to looking at the babies. These meetings were very successful. Staff attended well and became animated in thinking about the babies. All kinds of old and good practices that had been eroded were discussed again as if they were fresh ideas. Doctors and nurses talked together about how much intervention a particular baby could put up with and whether the nurses could retrieve their role as spokespersons for the babies and tell the doctors when it was not a good time to be doing some procedure.

The use of video in this way is interesting. It gives staff the opportunity to look at the babies without having to be responsible for doing something at that moment. These are small meetings, and so staff often feel free to talk about thoughts they had not articulated before—and the idea that exploring their own responses is useful can be a liberation. Of course, like everything else on the NICU, the enterprise can go the other way: the camera can be used as a defence against or distancing from the baby's experience. The person holding the camera can begin to hone in on particular aspects of the baby, thus directing the viewer's thoughts, or there can be a wish to get "good" shots or dramatic footage, so that an element of journalism enters. If these attitudes prevail, the original intention is foiled.

In our first meeting we considered a baby, "Jacob", who was doing well. This baby was one of twins. His twin had died *in utero*; the mother had gone on for seven and a half weeks carrying one live and one dead baby and had delivered at nearly 30 weeks' gestation. Jacob had the usual ups and downs of a premature baby who is doing fairly well. In the meantime, the parents were grieving for the dead baby. All of this was reiterated in the group, and we got on with watching the video. The experience of watching a baby on video is always very powerful. On the whole, the nurses deal well with the recognition that the lights are too bright, that there is too much noise, that too much is being done to the babies. With Jacob, the circumstances did not seem too unbearable, and there was a lively discussion about improving practice. There were some thoughts of his dead twin—about which sex it had been, and whether Jacob was missing it. The thought that twins should not be separated came up. There was some lively discussion between the nurses and a junior doctor about what could be seen on the video—whether one could really see that the baby was missing his twin. This led to a more general discussion about the meaning behind behaviour and how we can interpret what we see. There was some productive disagreement about the state Jacob was in—whether some manageable struggling was helpful for him, whether we should be trying to protect him from all difficulty, or whether if he managed to recover himself this was perhaps a strengthening and developing experience for him. The group of four—that is the two child psychotherapists and the two speech and language therapists—discussed this disagreement afterwards, and we thought that we should articulate before the next meeting that we welcomed disagreement and were not saying that there was only one way of interpreting what was going on for the baby, that what we valued was looking and thinking.

When we watched the video of Jacob the following week, we were struck by the beauty of his hand movements. It made us wonder what his feet would be like if they were uncovered and we could see them properly. We saw even more of his tremendous capacity to recover himself from more disintegrated states. As we watched, one very senior nurse was having a very bad coughing fit, which was actually an asthma attack. The other child psychotherapist and I both turned to her with concern and offered her a drink of water. She recovered and went on to talk passionately about various practices that could be improved—for instance, her dislike of Q-tips and her feeling that a little piece of cotton wool was better, and what kind of medication was preferable for reflux. It made me wonder about the identification of this nurse, and the nurses generally, with the babies. Dr Gibbons and I had always thought that the staff need to be attended to in order to be helped to attend to the babies—an idea that is really at the heart of staff support. Here it seemed that when the baby was being attended to, the nurse nearly suffocated until some consideration was shown to her, and then she recovered and thought with some identification about the baby.

The group was very interested in Jacob and his mother and the sight of something very beautiful. We watched the mother cleaning her baby and talking to him. We wondered about her different attitude to his top half and his bottom half. She seemed to become less intimate when she turned to his bottom half. But then she was delighted when Jacob defecated, because he had been constipated. She stroked his thigh with great tenderness. There was some idea that she was delighted with his genitals, maybe with this strong surviving boy—the parents felt sure that his twin had been a girl.

At the end of this meeting we talked about what we should do next time. The senior nurse thought that we should watch a video of a very sick baby in the hot nursery who was not doing well. I wondered whether there was a sense that we had had the pleasure of enjoying Jacob and thinking and talking about him, and now we should think about a less fortunate mother and baby. It might also have been that sometimes we find it easier to look at the less fortunate—that the sight of a very loving happy mother with a beautiful responding baby can fire our envy—as described in chapter 6—especially when it is done with such bravery in the face of such odds. We might say, what right does she have to be so happy? There were worries about videoing the more deprived mother, about whether she would be able to tolerate it. And it was agreed to leave this to the speech therapist and the child psychotherapist to decide.

The next time we did discuss this sicker baby. More doctors attended, and the following time one of the consultants came. It felt as if something good was happening in the middle of all of this bad feeling, and that it was something that had the babies very much in focus.

In the meantime one of the consultants, Dr Kennedy, became worried about the morale of the nurses. Dr Gibbons and I had been hearing from nurses how worried they were for their jobs, about what would happen if there was a merger, whether there was going to be a merger. There was a lot of anger that a nurse manager had left without saying goodbye, without addressing these issues, and only came to the nurses individually with a complaint from a mother. So we arranged that Dr Kennedy would attend a regular staff support meeting to answer questions, and we hoped other senior people would come. We put up a notice about this. There was an angry reaction on the unit. We were asked by another consultant to cancel the meeting, "to pour oil on troubled waters". The meeting was cancelled. But some senior nurses came and again voiced discontent and worry about whether there would be jobs for them, a fury that the unit was being down-graded, and a sense of humiliation that Hospital C was now a better unit. They felt that they had been through bad times before, but with hard work and pulling together they had got through. Now they felt that no one was rooting for the unit. Underlying this was anger with the unit manager and the feeling that she was not championing the unit, that she was only too pleased that it was being downgraded because of her worries about staffing levels and safety. But this was not clearly articulated by the nurses at the meeting. Once again it was agreed that there needed to be a meeting with the consultants and the manager, but that this time it would not be specially advertised, it would just take place at the usual meeting in two weeks' time.

In the intervening week we had a staff support meeting. Dr Gibbons and I had just learnt that there had been a tribunal about a senior nurse. It had not been completed and had been postponed. Two doctors, "Graham" and "David", walked in. Graham said that things were picking up on the unit—four new nurses had been offered jobs. It was not yet known if they would accept. I asked if the transitional nursery might be reopened. Halfway there, said Graham. Dr Gibbons mentioned the morale of the nurses. Graham replied very tentatively that there was a hearing. We both said that we had heard about this. Graham went on to say that this nurse had been difficult to work with, the atmosphere was often bad when she was on duty, and the hearing had been deferred for about a month. Dr Gibbons mentioned that even the doctors noticed that the atmosphere with this particular nurse was bad.

At this point a nurse, Julie, walked in. We told her what we were talking about. Julie said that Alex, the nurse who was suspended, was a first-class nurse—very good. Dr Gibbons said, well, he hoped that she was and is—that is, that she was still alive. Marcia, a junior nurse, walked in with her lunch. Julie said that they were not allowed to contact Alex, and she was not allowed to contact them. We asked who had said that. Julie said that her name and her telephone number had been crossed off the duty list. I said that that was because she was not coming to work at the moment and could not be called on to do extra shifts, but no one had said that she must not be spoken to, had they? Julie said that both her name and her telephone number had been blocked out. I asked if this was done so that it could not be read, and Julie said it was. I said that it sounded like Trotsky being blocked out of Soviet photographs as if he had never existed, that this seemed to go back to Dr Gibbons' remark about whether Alex was still alive.

This led to some thought about how isolated Alex might feel. Julie repeated that she was a first-class nurse. She was an outsider, and she had got this job over three insiders, so she had got a lot of grief when she started work here. Two of these passed-over nurses had left, but there was already an atmosphere against her. Dr Gibbons said that this was very interesting, quite another point of view—that Julie was saying that her behaviour was a reaction to a campaign against her.

Julie agreed and said that it was a reaction and that it was to do with things being very unprofessional around here. Marcia looked up from tucking into her lunch and said, "Amen, Sister." Julie said that there was a lot of racism and unprofessional behaviour. I asked Marcia what she meant, and she said that she was agreeing with Julie. She had had a miserable time here, and she had been thinking of asking for a transfer to paediatrics. Josie, a senior sister, had asked to see her, had given her some time and talked to her about the pros and cons, and had asked her to wait a bit. She had really appreciated that, and she would wait. But when she had first come, she was just a student. She had had a baby. Her mind was different after having the baby. She had lost her marbles. Dr Gibbons said that he thought you needed different marbles after having a baby. He asked Marcia when she had had the baby. She counted up and said that she had begun work here when the baby was 3 months old. We asked her whether she had had to—perhaps that was rather hard. But her face lit up, and she said that she had very much wanted to—a new job! But she had only just finished being a student when she started here, and she had been called into the manager's office. Everyone knew about it. I said that it must have been humiliating, and Marcia said that it was. She said that everyone makes mistakes, but more senior people know how to hide them. I asked her if she had a mentor or anyone to turn to. Marcia and Julie said that they have preceptors whose job is to advise you, but they do not really work with you, they do not really know you. Dr Gibbons emphasized that this support system did not seem to work. I asked what happened with their teams. Julie explained that the teams were not there to support the nurses, they just had particular babies assigned to them. I asked if they might actually be nursing other babies, and Julie said that they might be. Graham commented that they have those red, green and blue teams. Julie agreed. He asked how one knows which team a baby belongs to, and Julie said that the files were different colours. Everyone laughed at such a simple explanation. There was some disagreement about whether the membership of these teams was written up on a board. It was said that it was not, because they did not want it to be too obvious to the parents. Someone said that the names were written in different colours if the pens were there. And there was more laughter this time at the haphazard nature of the organization.

Dr Gibbons said that he had thought that I was going to ask why Marcia had not come to staff support when she felt so unsupported—that we had had only an inkling of these rows, but that people had not brought them to us.

Julie said that the people who caused this bad atmosphere were chameleons: they were green with one and red with another. They came to staff support, but they would not talk about these things. Dr Gibbons said that staff support did not seem adequate to deal with these things. He said that there seemed to be a lot of bitchiness about: men might get angry in different ways from women, more a kind of playground stuff. Marcia agreed, but Dr Gibbons mistakenly thought that she was criticizing him. She corrected him and agreed with him, saying that where there were a lot of women, there was bitchiness.

I said that I wondered about all of these quarrels, and whether they were connected to having to work with such sick babies, who were often in a lot of pain. Graham looked rather sceptical. Marcia said that she had swallowed and swallowed—and swallowed so much stuff, but now she would not any more, and she felt better. Julie then talked about swallowing a lot.

There was some laughter about swallowing so much. I wondered if the mothers had to swallow a lot: they had to be polite, because they wanted the staff to be kind to their babies; they had to swallow so much, having to let other people handle their babies and having to walk out of the unit and leave their babies behind. I thought that many of them must hate what was happening to them, and then they swallowed their hatred.

Julie agreed and said that they swallow and swallow and then they blow up, and everyone is surprised. She said that it had happened on the unit just the other day. A mother had swallowed so much, and then she blew up about quite a small thing. I said that there was an awful lot of swallowing, and Dr Gibbons said that perhaps the babies were having to do quite a lot of swallowing too.

Graham got called out on his bleep, and soon it was time for us to finish. There was some more talk about Alex, the nurse who had been suspended. Julie told us that she no longer worked Bank shifts. These are run by an internal nursing agency. She had had a row with the Bank management because they had not paid her for nine weeks. In the end the manager here had paid her out of unit finance. But she was then told to work things out with Bank herself, and there was some idea that the unit manager would be pleased if she left. Dr Gibbons said that it was clear that she was a troublemaker.

Several things seemed apparent afterwards. Graham was very keen that things should be all right, he felt that unit life was improving, and that there could be some laughter. But Julie and Marcia had a different point of view. They left us wondering whether Alex had been scapegoated, loaded with everyone's cruelty and bullying and driven out, or whether she was the boil that had to be lanced, as someone put it. We felt continually as if we did not know what was going on, as if we were children kept out of the secret. But as the meeting went on, we heard about how this cruelty had been put out in an inaccessible place, onto the nurse who was said to have treated her juniors viciously, and that there was a great wish to deny its existence. It seems that this state leads to nurses feeling very unlooked-after. When Marcia talked about her own baby, Dr Gibbons and I were quick to think about the baby and to feel that 3 months was too young for a baby to be left by its mother. Maybe this made the group feel unlooked-after by us— that we are always thinking about the babies the nurses have to look after rather than thinking about their baby selves. Perhaps at this moment we have the wrong "marbles". Certainly it seems that the nurses are saying that the babies are provided for, but they are not—the colour coding is for the babies not for the nurses, and the provisions that should be in place are not working. Maybe there is an idea that Dr Gibbons and I do not know the nurses.

I think that Dr Gibbons was getting to that when he said that he thought that I was going to ask them why they had not brought these conflicts to staff support meetings, but I had asked about other provisions for them. Perhaps the feeling was that I wanted to hand them on to someone else, not wanting to bother with the infantile feelings of the group myself. It seemed that there was a competition between the staff and the babies about who was going to be looked after. At this point the idea arose about the difference between men and women. Maybe the thought was that men might not be so clued in, but they were also not so cruel. I think that I enacted that and made an interpretation about how disturbing these sick babies were to everyone and that that was why they were quarrelling. Graham looked sceptical, but the nurses went on to talk about swallowing and swallowing. I wondered whether they felt that I was ramming the babies down their throats, as if there was no room for themselves, as if they were only being serviced in order to get them back to the babies. At that time there was a baby in the unit whose mother thought that he might play for Arsenal, while the staff wondered whether he would ever sit up. Some nurses were critical of the mother, that she did not do more of the care for the baby. I wondered whether nurses were feeling that the babies were just too much to look after. Perhaps there was a sense of being burdened by these babies and not being recognized themselves, that they were just there to do this job. Dr Gibbons pointed out that the babies themselves might be having to do a lot of swallowing. He was thinking of painful intubation and the remark of the nurse a few weeks previously that it was like Armageddon. But the nurses did not want to think about this. The meeting seemed to tail away with this story about the manager wanting Julie to leave.

I think that we failed to take up a sense of our cruelty. It seems that the propaganda was that we were cruel to want the nurses and doctors to be in touch with infantile needs—whether these were their own or the babies'—and that it was much better to be in the throes of more masturbatory excitement about the intrigues of unit life. We could think of this excitement as bitching, but it was actually so cruel that people began to feel that their working lives were intolerable. What was remarkable was how the nurses, quite powerful professional people, seemed to become drawn into the cruelty, either by perpetrating it or by succumbing to it, perhaps in the latter case in identification with the babies' helplessness.

Our next meeting a week later was arranged so that the consultants could be present. Both Dr Gibbons and I were there. Three consultants attended, the unit manager and an SHO who had been pulled in by one of the consultants. But no nurses came. I felt very foolish at this lack of turnout. We talked about what this lack of communication might be about, about how bad things had become. The doctors began to use the meeting to ask the SHO about what could be changed to make things better for the junior doctors. Although I was relieved that the meeting was being used in some way, I felt that we were getting away from the task. Towards the end, the registrar came in. He had been quite openly against staff support meetings. He suggested that they should take place less often: that it was nice for the doctors to be able to go and have lunch together. Dr Gibbons said that that would be the beginning of the end—that nobody would remember, and the continuity would be lost. The registrar said that a baby had died at the weekend, but none of the staff who were involved would be at work on Tuesday, when the next staff support meeting would be. Dr Kennedy made an impassioned speech about the need to meet—she remembered a time when she was a junior doctor when feelings had to go unacknowledged and unlooked-after. She said it was up to senior doctors to make sure that people could come, that staff were often happy to come in for such a meeting even in their own free time. She went on to say that they might not appreciate these meetings now, but when doctors came back, having been elsewhere, where there were no such meetings, they said how much they appreciated them. All of this was rather directed at the registrar. Both Dr Gibbons and I talked about the bad state the unit was in and the way that staff support was not being used. Senior doctors told us afterwards that they were worried about this kind of talk, lest it should put junior doctors off coming to work here. We all continued talking about the viability of the staff support meetings, and the fact that a baby had died was lost.

The following week Dr Gibbons could not be present, so I took the staff support meeting alone. This time it was packed with senior nurses who reiterated their worries about whether there were going to be jobs for them, whether they were going to come in and find that this was their last day. They complained that their manager was saying that nothing was going to happen, whereas a consultant was saying that there was definitely going to be a merger. We talked about how they had not come to the meeting with the consultants, how difficult it seemed to be to get together or to get questions answered. They said that as nurses, they hated confrontation. It seemed that their anger was such that they thought that no one could put up with it.

In some ways, matters then improved. It was decided that the suspended nurse should return to work, and much thought was given to promoting her reintegration. The intermediary nursery reopened, and three new nurses were hired. There seemed to be a renewed interest in work. But the hospital Accident and Emergency Unit again hit the headlines, with all the ensuing sense of persecution for all departments, and for the hospital in general.

These are recurrently difficult situations, and different defences are brought into play against them. Of course, this has its effect on Dr Gibbons and on me too. We sometimes find ourselves wanting to retire, to hand over to someone else, and with that comes the fear of retiring, of becoming depressed, and, of course, of old age and dying. Sometimes we hope that no one will turn up to staff support meetings, and then we can talk to each other. We may lapse into the feeling that there is a mystery in the unit conflicts, that there are good guys and bad guys and that we could align ourselves along this division. I think that we both feel that we could not have done this support work singly, that we would have become disheartened and given up. We have had each other to talk to, in trying to make sense of things. We have also thought that it is better for the staff that they have the two of us to come to—that we are more robust than either would be on their own. When they

come straggling in, full of ambivalence, they come to something
that is already quite lively rather than to an individual worn out by
their neglect

I have lived rather like an anthropologist in this very self-con-
tained tribe. My main feeling is of gratitude and affection to this
community of colleagues, staff, parents, and babies. My hope is
that my eyes and thoughts have been helpful. Insofar as I have
known about the kinds of defences people have assumed, I have
known about them through internal acquaintance.

> Man is surely mad with discontent, he is hurled
> By lovely hopes or bad dreams against the world,
>
> ·   ·   ·   ·   ·   ·   ·   ·   ·
>
> Conscious of guilt and vast inadequacy and the sick
> Ego and the broken past and the clock that goes too quick,
> Conscious of waste of labour, conscious of spite and hate,
> Of dissension with his neighbour, of beggars at the gate,
> But conscious also of love and the joy of things and the power
> Of going beyond and above the limits of the lagging hour,
> Conscious of sunlight, conscious of death's inveigling touch,
> Not completely conscious but partly—and that is much.

Louis MacNeice, "Plurality" (August 1940)

GLOSSARY

This is an extended glossary that may be of interest to the non-medical reader.

Apnoea: a pause in the breathing pattern; **apnoea attacks:** episodes in which breathing is interrupted; **apnoea alarm:** machine to warn the staff of a pause in the baby's breathing pattern.

Aspiration: inhalation of fluid (stomach juices, mucus, milk) into the lungs; it but can also designate the use of a suction device to draw fluids out of the lungs.

Blood gases: laboratory test to measure levels of oxygen and carbon dioxide in the blood.

BM Stix: a test requiring a small drop of blood, to check the level of glucose in the blood.

Bradycardia: an abnormal slowing of the heartbeat.

Brain scan: use of ultrasound to obtain information about the brain.

Chronic lung disease: indicated by continuing need of oxygen after forty weeks of age.

CPAP: Continuous positive airway pressure—a way of helping babies who only need a little assistance with breathing.

D&C: short for *dilation and curettage*—procedure for clearing superfluous tissue from the uterus.

Endotracheal tube (ETT): plastic tube inserted through the mouth into the windpipe. Assists breathing and also allows removal of secretions.

Epidural: short for *epidural anaesthetic*—by injection to lower part of spinal canal.

Headbox: clear Perspex box placed over the baby's head to assist oxygen delivery.

IA line: intra-arterial line = a line for taking blood samples from an artery, usually in the wrist or ankle.

Mask ventilation: method of assisting breathing: a small, soft mask is placed over the face, and a mixture of air and oxygen flows into it from the ventilator.

Nasal prong: a way of delivering CPAP through a tube in the nose.

Nasogastric feeds: the giving of feed via a fine, soft tube passed through the nose into the stomach.

Nasojejunal feed: the giving of feeds via a fine, soft tube (**nasojejunal tube, NJT**) passed through the nose, through the stomach, and on into the upper part of the small intestine. The stomach remains empty, reducing the likelihood of regurgitation or vomiting.

Pneumothorax: presence of air between the lung and the chest wall, which sometimes interferes with breathing.

Reflux: the flowing back of stomach fluid into the oesophagus.

Senior House Officer (SHO): Junior doctor.

Tracheostomy: surgical opening in the trachea—the passage connecting the larynx and the windpipe (bronchi).

Total parenteral nutrition (TPN): supplying all essential nutrients for growth by infusion into a vein.

Umbilical catheter (UAC): a tube passed through the umbilical cord to help feed and monitor the baby.

Ventilation: mechanical aid to assist breathing, so that the baby can achieve normal levels of oxygen in the blood.

REFERENCES AND BIBLIOGRAPHY

Als, H. (1986). A synactive model of neonatal behavioural organisa-
tion: framework for the assessment and support of the neural–
behavioural development of the premature infant and his parent
in the environment of the neonatal intensive care unit. In: J. K.
Sweeney (Ed.), *The High-Risk Newborn: Developmental Therapy Per-
spectives. Physical and Occupational Therapy in Paediatrics*. Bingham-
ton, NY: Haworth Press.

Anand, K. J. S. (1987). Randomised trial of fentanyl anaesthesia in preterm babies undergoing surgery: effects on the stress response. *The
Lancet, 11*: 243–247.

Baxandall, M. (1972). *Painting and Experience in Fifteenth Century Italy*.
Oxford: Oxford University Press.

Bender, H. (1990). On the outside looking in: sibling perceptions,
dreams and fantasies of the premature infant. *International Journal
of Prenatal and Perinatal Studies*, 133–143.

Benjamin, W. (1999). *The Storyteller: Illuminations*. London: Pimlico.

Bick, E. (1964). Notes on infant observation in psycho-analytic training. *International Journal of Psycho-Analysis, 5*: 558–566.

Bick, E. (1968). The experience of the skin in early object relations.
International Journal of Psycho-Analysis, 49: 484–486.

Bion, W. R. (1959). Attacks on linking. *International Journal of Psycho-
Analysis, 40* (5–6): 308.

213

Bion, W. R. (1961). *Experiences in Groups*. London: Tavistock Publications.

Bion, W. R. (1962). *Learning from Experience*. London: Heinemann.

Bion, W. R. (1967). *Second Thoughts*. London: Heinemann.

Bion, W. R. (1970). *Attention and Interpretation*. London: Tavistock Publications.

Black, D. (1996). Childhood bereavement. *British Medical Journal, 312* (15 June): 1496.

Bowlby, J. (1973). *Attachment and Loss, Vol. 2: Separation, Anxiety and Anger*. New York: Basic Books.

Brazelton, T. B. (1973). *Neonatal Behavioural Assessment Scale*. Philadelphia, PA: Lippincott; London: Blackwell, 1984.

Brazelton, T., & Cramer, B. (1991). *The Earliest Relationship*. London: Karnac.

Brazelton, T. B., Kolowski, B., & Main, M. (1974). The origins of reciprocity: the early mother–infant interaction. In: M. Lewis & L. A. Rosenblum (Eds.), *The Effects of the Infant on the Caregiver*. New York: Wiley.

Brazelton, T. B., Tronich, E., Adamson, L., Als, H., & Wise, S. (1975). *Early Mother–Infant Reciprocity in Parent–Infant Interaction*. North Holland: Ciba Foundation Symposium 33; New York & Amsterdam: Elsevier.

Bretherton, I. (1985). Attachment theory, retrospect and prospect. In: I. Bretherton & E. Waters, *Growing Points of Attachment Theory and Research*. SRCD Monographs, *50*: 3–35.

Butler, H. (1990). *The Sub-prefect Should Have Held His Tongue and Other Essays*, ed. R. Foster. London: Allen Lane/Penguin Press.

Clarke, D. A. (1994). Stress without distress: the intrauterine perspective. *The Lancet, 344* (July): 73–74.

Cornell, E. M., & Gottfried, A. W. (1976). Intervention with premature human infants. *Child Development, 47*: 32–39.

Dillner, L. (1992). Keeping babies in prison. *British Medical Journal, 304* (April): 932–933.

Eliot, G. (1876). *Middlemarch*. Harmondsworth: Penguin.

Field, T. M. (1990a). Neonatal stress and coping in intensive care. *Infant Mental Health Journal, 11*: 57–65.

Field, T. M. (1990b). Alleviating stress in newborn infants in the intensive care unit. *Clinics in Perinatology, 17*: 1–9.

Fletcher, A. (1983). Working in a neonatal intensive care unit. *Journal of Child Psychotherapy, 9*: 47–55.

Fraiberg, S. (1982). Pathological defenses in infancy. *Psychoanalytic Quarterly, 11*: 612–634.

Freud, S. (1936a). A disturbance of memory on the Acropolis. *Standard Edition, Vol. 22*, pp. 239–248.

Freud, W. E. (1989). Notes on some psychological aspects of neonatal intensive care. In: S. I. Greenspan & G. H. Pollock (Eds.), *The Case of Life, Vol. 1: Infancy*. Madison, WI: International Universities Press.

Giannakoulopoulis, X., et al. (1994). Fetal plasma cortisol and B-endorphin response to intrauterine needling. *The Lancet, 344* (July): 77–81.

Gorski, P. A. (1983). Premature infant behaviour and physiological response to caregiving intervention in the intensive care nursery. In: J. D. Call, E. Gallerson, & R. L. Tyson (Eds.), *Frontiers of Infant Psychiatry, Vol. 1*. New York: Basic Books.

Hale, R., & Hudson, L. (1992). The Tavistock Study of Young Doctors: report of the pilot phase. *British Journal of Hospital Medicine, 47* (6): 452–462.

Hampshire, S. (1951). *Spinoza*. Harmondsworth: Penguin Books.

Harris, M. (1987). *The Collected Papers of Martha Harris and Esther Bick*, ed. M. Harris Williams. Strathtay, Perthshire: Clunie Press.

Jones, M. A. (1989). Identifying signs that nurses interpret as indicating pain in newborns. *Paediatric Nursing, 15* (1): 76–79.

Judd, D. (1989). *Give Sorrow Words*. London: Free Association Books.

Klein, M. (1952). Notes on some schizoid mechanisms. In: *Developments in Psycho-Analysis*. London: Hogarth Press.

Klein, M. (1957). *Envy and Gratitude*. London: Tavistock Publications.

Levi, P. (1992). *The Drowned and the Saved*. London: Abacus.

MacNeice, L. (1966). *Plurality*. In: *Collected Poems* (p. 243). London & Boston, MA: Faber & Faber.

Marshall, R. E., & Kasman, C. (1980). Burnout in the neonatal intensive care unit. *Paediatric Medicine, 65* (6): 1161–1165.

McFadyen, A. (1994). *Special Care Babies and Their Developing Relationships*. London: Routledge.

McIntosh, N., Van Veen, L., & Bramweyer, H. (1993). The pain of heel prick and its management in preterm babies. *Pain, 52*: 71–74.

Meltzer, D. (1973). *Sexual States of Mind*. Strathtay, Perthshire: Clunie Press.

Meltzer, D. (1988). *The Apprehension of Beauty*. Strathtay, Perthshire: Clunie Press.

Menzies-Lyth, I. (1988). *Containing Anxiety in Institution*. London: Free Association Books.

Miller, I., Rustin, M., & Shuttleworth, J. (Eds.) (1989). *Closely Observed Infants*. London: Duckworth.

Minde, K. (1991). The effect of disordered parenting on the develop-
ment of children. In: M. Lewis (Ed.), *Child and Adolescent Psychiatry:
A Comprehensive Textbook* (pp. 394–401). Baltimore, MD: Williams
& Wilkins.

Minde, K., & Benoit, D. (1991). Infant psychiatry: its relevance for the
general psychiatrist. *British Journal of Psychiatry, 159*: 173–184.

Minde, K., & Stewart, D. (1988). Psychiatric services in the neo-natal
intensive care unit. In: R. Cohen (Ed.), *Psychiatric Consultation in
Childbirth Settings* (pp. 151–164). New York: Plenum.

Negri, R. (1994). *The Newborn in the Intensive Care Unit.* London: Karnac.

Newman, L. F. (1981). Social and sensory environment of low birth
weight infants in special care nursery. *Journal of Nervous and Mental
Diseases, 169*: 448–455.

Oakley, A. (1985). *The Captured Womb: History of the Medical Care of
Pregnant Women.* Oxford: Blackwell.

Oates, R. K., & Oates, P. (1995). Stress and mental health in neonatal
intensive care units. *Archives of Disease in Childhood, 72*: F107–F110.

Obholzer, A., & Roberts, V. Z. (Eds.) (1994). *The Unconscious at Work.*
London & New York: Routledge.

Piontelli, A. (1992). *From Foetus to Child: An Observational and Psychoanalytic Study.* London: Routledge.

Rachels, J. (1986). *The End of Life: The Morality of Euthanasia.* Oxford:
Oxford University Press.

Rennie, J. M. (1996). Perinatal management at the lower margin of
viability. *Archives of Disease in Childhood, 74*: F214–F218.

Rogers, M. C. (1992). Do the right thing: pain relief in infants and
children. *New England Journal of Medicine, 326*: 55–56.

Rosenblatt, J. B., & Redshaw, M. E. (1984). Factors influencing the
psychological adjustment of mothers to the birth of a preterm
infant. *Frontiers of Infant Psychiatry, Vol. 11.* New York: Basic Books.

Stern, D. N. (1985). *The Interpersonal World of the Infant.* New York:
Basic Books.

Stern, M., & Karraker, K. M. (1990). The prematurity stereotype: em-
pirical evidence and implications for practice. *Infant Medical Health
Journal, 11*: 3–11.

Szur, R. (1981). Infants in hospital (Hospital care of the newborn: some
aspects of personal stress). *Journal of Child Psychotherapy, 7*: 137–
140.

Turnock, C. (1997). ICU syndrome: a discussion of the effects of intensive care on critically ill patients. *British Journal of Intensive Care*
(July–August): 144–147.

Valman, H. B., & Pearson, J. F. (1980). The first year of life: what the fetus feels. *British Medical Journal, 280* (26 Jan., No. 6209): 233–234.

Verny, T., & Kelly, J. (1981). *The Secret Life of the Unborn Child.* London: Summit Books.

Winnicott, D. (1965). *The Maturational Processes and the Facilitating Environment.* New York: International Universities Press.

Wollheim, R. (1984). *The Thread of Life.* Cambridge: Cambridge University Press.

Yeats, W. B. (1919). *The Second Coming.* In: *Collected Poems* (pp. 210–211). London: Macmillan, 1950.

INDEX